NEW ORLEANS BY NIGHT

Frommer's

NEW ORLEANS
by Night

BY

MICHAEL TISSERAND

A BALLIETT & FITZGERALD BOOK

MACMILLAN • USA

a disclaimer

Prices fluctuate in the course of time, and travel information changes under the impact of the varied and volatile factors that influence the travel industry. Neither the author nor the publisher can be held responsible for the experiences of readers while traveling. Readers are invited to write to the publisher with ideas, comments, and suggestions for future editions.

about the author

Michael Tisserand is a freelance writer whose work has appeared in the *Washington Post, USA Today, and Billboard.* In New Orleans, he has been an associate editor for *Gambit Weekly* and a columnist for *OffBeat,* and he has received two New Orleans Press Club awards. He is also the author of an upcoming book about zydeco music. While he's never taken a room at the Hummingbird Hotel & Grill, he's nodded off in the booths a couple of times.

Balliett & Fitzgerald, Inc.
Executive editor: Tom Dyja
Managing editor: Duncan Bock
Associate editor: Howard Slatkin
Assistant editor: Maria Fernandez
Editorial assistants: Ruth Ro, Bindu Poulose, Donna Spillane

Macmillan Travel art director: Michele Laseau

All maps © Simon & Schuster, Inc.

MACMILLAN TRAVEL
A Simon & Schuster Macmillan Company
1633 Broadway
New York, NY 10019

ISBN 0-02-861333-3
Library of Congress information available from Library of Congress.

special sales

Bulk purchases (10+ copies) of Frommer's and selected Macmillan travel guides are available to corporations, organizations, institutions, and charities at special discounts, and can be customized to suit individual needs. For more information write to Special Sales, Macmillan General Reference, 1633 Broadway, New York, NY 10019.

Manufactured in the United States of America

contents

New Orleans Orientation

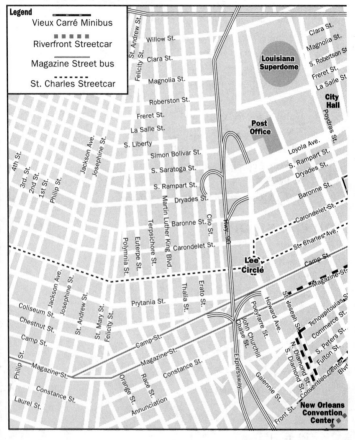

Legend

Vieux Carré Minibus

Riverfront Streetcar

Magazine Street bus

St. Charles Streetcar

St. Andrew St.

Willow St.

Felicity St.

Clara St.

Magnolia St.

Roberston St.

Freret St.

La Salle St.

S. Liberty

Simon Bolivar St.

S. Saratoga St.

S. Rampart St.

Dryades St.

Baronne St.

Clio St.

Carondelet St.

Jackson Ave.

Josephine St.

4th St.

3rd. St.

2nd St.

1st St.

Philip St.

Martin Luther King Blvd.

Terpsichore St.

Euterpe St.

Polymnia St.

Erato St.

Thalia St.

Prytania St.

Jackson Ave.

Josephine St.

St. Andrew St.

St. Mary St.

Felicity St.

Coliseum St.

Chestnut St.

Camp St.

Philip St.

Magazine St.

Constance St.

Laurel St.

Orange St.

Race St.

Annunciation

Camp St.

Magazine St.

Constance St.

Clara St.

Magnolia St.

S. Robertson St.

Freret St.

La Salle St.

Louisiana Superdome

City Hall

Poydras St.

Post Office

Loyola Ave.

S. Rampart St.

Dryades St.

Baronne St.

Carondelet St.

St. Charles Ave.

Camp St.

Lee Circle

Magazine St.

Howard Ave.

Poeyfarre St.

John Churchill Chase St.

St. Joseph St.

N. Diamond St.

S. Diamond St.

Galennie St.

Front St.

Expressway

Hwy. 90

Tchoupitoulas St.

Commerce St.

S. Peters St.

Fulton St.

Convention Center Blvd.

New Orleans Convention Center

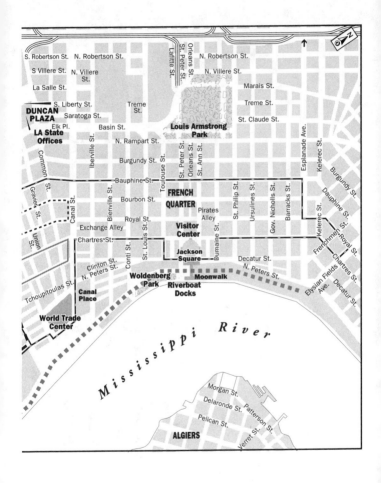

S. Robertson St. N. Robertson St. N. Robertson St.

S Villere St. N. Villere St.

La Salle St. Treme St. Marais St.

S. Liberty St. Treme St.

DUNCAN PLAZA Saratoga St. St. Claude St.

LA State Offices Elk Pl. Basin St. **Louis Armstrong Park**

Iberville St. N. Rampart St.

Common St. Burgundy St. Toulouse St.

Dauphine St. Esplanade Ave.

Gravier St. Bienville St. Bourbon St. **FRENCH QUARTER** St. Philip St. Ursulines St. Gov. Nicholls St. Barracks St. Kelerec St.

Canal St. Royal St. Pirates Alley Burgundy St.

Union St. Exchange Alley St. Louis St. **Visitor Center** Dumaine St. Kelerec St. Dauphine St.

Chartres St. Frenchmen-Royal St.

Conti St. **Jackson Square** Decatur St.

Clinton St. N. Peters St. N. Peters St. Chartres St.

Tchoupitoulas St. **Woldenberg Park** **Moonwalk** Elysian Fields Ave. Decatur St.

Canal Place **Riverboat Docks**

World Trade Center

Mississippi River

Morgan St.

Delaronde St. Patterson St.

Pelican St. Verret St.

ALGIERS

what's
hot,
what's
not

New Orleanians don't co-opt fads, we create them—or so we like to believe. From the hot soundtrack of the Jazz Age to the hot food of the Cajun craze, the Crescent City has long supplied the continent with both cuisine and culture.

Fittingly, what's hot in New Orleans right now is New Orleans. Theater patrons prefer plays that either satirize or celebrate home-town life. Locals groove to music that is steeped in the local scene—we have a seemingly limitless appetite for repeated renditions of "Iko-Iko" and "Hey Pocky Way." And in the age of health consciousness, New Orleanians still prefer New Orleans food, in all its deep-fried, sauce-drenched glory.

A traveler through the city (and through these pages) will discover that the past few years have wrought their changes. Chain stores, bars, and restaurants now offer stiff competition to home-grown favorites, and a gargantuan downtown casino may or may not alter the cityscape as it now stands. You can even order a salad in many local diners. Yet these are cosmetic changes: New Orleans is still about gumbo, zydeco, homespun libations, and large portions of it all.

Approach the Big Easy with a big appetite. Dinner in the French Quarter is the natural place to start; following that, Bourbon Street is tacky, but it's worth a walk. Hot jazz clubs lie on the parameter of the Quarter, and the House of Blues usually has a "name" artist, often with Louisiana ties. If you want to venture out into the city, check out the Warehouse District rock clubs, the Mid-City Lanes (in Mid-City, of course), and the Uptown bar scene; then close out the night at a 24-hour breakfast dive, or dive back into the Quarter for beignets at the Cafe Du Monde. Through it all, follow this rule of thumb: if you think you've whetted your appetite, you're not done yet.

What's hot

Yet another jazz renaissance... The birthplace of Louis Armstrong is also the wellspring of some of the hottest sounds in contemporary jazz. Wynton and Branford Marsalis' younger brothers Delfeayo and Jason are making their marks. Wess Anderson and Jeremy Davenport are two more young lions on the scene, and trumpeter Nicholas Payton is gaining new recognition with a featured role in the Robert Altman film *Kansas City*, scheduled for release in 1996. You can catch these guys in some of the most prestigious clubs and concert halls in the world, or you can hear them in New Orleans in neighborhood joints such as

Donna's, **New Showcase Lounge**, and **Funky Butt**, as well as the more established **Snug Harbor** (see The Club Scene). The city is finally taking official notice of the scene, and plans are being bandied about to revitalize Rampart Street and nearby Armstrong Park, and possibly create a jazz museum. But nobody's holding their breath, especially the trumpet players.

Rockin' to New Orleans... Having been a major force in the jazz age and in the golden era of R&B, this city is now finding itself in the age of big label rock bands. Among the local acts that have signed to the majors: Cowboy Mouth, James Hall, Anders Osborne, Better Than Ezra, Deadeye Dick, the Iguanas, and the rapper Mystikal. Up-and-coming bands to check out include the Continental Drifters, Galactic, the Boondoggles, and the Bingemen. For hot clubs, try the newly enlarged **Howlin' Wolf**, along with **Tipitina's** and **Rendon Inn** (see The Club Scene). In 1996, even the Jazz Fest embraced the rock scene, and booked national alternative favorites such as Phish and the Dave Matthews Band.

Dance, dance, dance... Three local dance scenes are hotter than ever. On Wednesdays and Thursdays, crowds pack into **Mid–City Lanes** to hear zydeco bands such as Beau Jocque and Rosie Ledet. It's all couple dancing, and just about everyone here will want to show you how to do it (especially the owner). Brass bands such as Rebirth, Treme, and the Soul Rebels play nightly at **Donna's**, as well as in second-line parades and festivals throughout the city. These all-horn bands combine trad jazz with hip-hop and reggae, and draw a young crowd. And the corner of Bourbon and St. Ann streets is the place to go for house and disco. **Oz** and **Parade** are both here, and this predominantly gay scene is attracting more and more straights (see The Club Scene).

Talk, talk, talk... The newest dens for debate, dialogue, and discourse are funky hipster bars such as **Snake and Jake Christmas Club Lounge** and the **R Bar** (see The Bar Scene). Time itself seems to stop once you sink into the couches and easy chairs, and then sink even deeper into conversation. The R Bar's decor is thrift store chic; Snake and Jake's is just thrift store. Both places keep the juke box at rocking decibels, so be prepared to shout your innermost thoughts at the top of your lungs. Or take it outside: on most nights, the crowds outsize the rooms and spill onto the sidewalk. For more sober talk, coffeeshops are finally starting to hit it big in the Big Easy, especially **Kaldi's** and **Rue deLa Course II** (see Hanging Out).

Good sports... Orleanians are being sent happily to the minors. The minor-league baseball **New Orleans Zephyrs** is the most satisfying spectator sport in town. The Z's will soon be breaking in a new, state-of-the-art facility, but many of the team's fans will miss the old lakeside diamond at University of New Orleans. The **New Orleans Riverboat Gamblers**, a minor league soccer team that plays at City Park, is also building a local fan base (see Sports).

Scary ghost stories... Just as the creepy voodoo movie *Angel Heart* was fading from memory, the creepy vampire movie *Interview with the Vampire* hit the screens, giving New Orleans still more notoriety for nefarious necromancy. Vampire author Anne Rice lives here, and her black-clad fans make pilgrimages to visit the settings of her spooky novels. (Check out Joy Dickinson's *Haunted City: An Unauthorized Guide to the Magical, Magnificent New Orleans of Anne Rice*.) Ghost and vampire tours are also springing to life around the French Quarter; **Magic Walking Tours** is a good opportunity for some late-night chills (see Hanging Out).

What's not

Tumbling dice... Build it and they will come, right? At press time, that old maxim was being refuted by a giant skeleton of a casino sitting half-finished in downtown New Orleans. From the start, Harrah's temporary facility in the Municipal Auditorium drew underwhelming crowds, and schemes to build the world's biggest casino went at least temporarily bust. Meanwhile, the citizens of Louisiana elected a new governor, largely due to his anti-gambling positions. There's talk that the whole gambling package—the state lottery, video poker, casino riverboats, and the land-based casino—may, for the first time, be put to a vote. This stuff will be running through the courts for years, but local governments and civic promoters are finally figuring out what most tourists already know: people don't come to New Orleans to spend the night at a slot machine.

Celebrity-owned chains... Locals watched warily as the chains started to move in on the French Quarter. First to arrive was **Jimmy Buffett's Margaritaville Cafe**. The gift shop had a few too many tropical shirts, but it all seemed harmless enough. Then the **House of Blues**—owned by Dan Aykroyd, Jim Belushi, and members of Aerosmith, among others—came to town. As the Neville Brothers and other top local groups began to play the House, locals worried that this might be the end of their beloved Tipitina's; but although that fine and funky music club was hit hard, it has survived. Others grumbled about the House's over-officious employees. But faced with a talent roster like Bob Dylan, Eric Clapton, Fats Domino, and Jerry Lee Lewis, even the loudest whiners eventually paid up and went inside. Then came the Night of the Living Four Shareholders: Sylvester Stallone, Bruce Willis, Arnold Schwarzenegger, and Demi Moore blew into town to open up **Planet Hollywood**. French Quarter residents had to wonder what was next for their neighborhood—a restaurant owned by leggy supermodels? Yes, **Fashion Cafe** soon opened across the street from Planet Hollywood. The transformation of this corner of the French Quarter into Creole Disneyland was complete, and some locals began to wax nostalgic for the days when this neighborhood was mainly old, abandoned buildings.

Celebrity sightings... The real New Orleans way to acknowledge international celebrities is to honestly not recognize them. The next best thing is to ignore them. This town has mastered the art of being too cool to care, which is one reason why celebs hang out here a little longer and later than they do in most cities. So when Bruce Springsteen stopped by the **Maple Leaf** for a drink, he stayed around and hopped on stage with the Iguanas. When Robert Plant joined the Soul Rebels and started doing some calls and responses with the crowd, some in the brass band wondered who this guy was, and if they should just ask him nicely to return to his seat. But the quintessential New Orleans attitude toward fame was expressed by the woman who works the door at **Mid-City Lanes**: When Mick Jagger stopped by the bowling alley to hear some zydeco, she chased after the entourage to remind them that the cover was $5.

Major league sports... We can't seem to get them, and we're not too wild about the ones we have. Efforts to attract an NBA franchise to town have yet to even hit the backboard. Meanwhile, it's hard not to harp on our one big-league pro team, the **New Orleans Saints** football franchise, who keep turning in less than heavenly seasons. At the start of each year, they're hot; by the end, they're not. Ticket scalpers start selling their best seats for face value. Fans pull paper bags over their heads, and callers to the sports talk shows go berserk with suggestions. No wonder the Louisiana Philharmonic Orchestra is doing so well.

Street music... The musicians who got their start on the streets of New Orleans form an impressive list, including Jimmy Buffett, the Rebirth Brass Band, and bluesman Corey Harris. Street entertainment has long been a major draw in the French Quarter, especially on Jackson Square and Royal Street. But in the early summer of 1996, the police began to crack down on the entertainers, citing infractions such as disturbing the peace, obstructing the sidewalk, and being too loud. At press time, all sides were trying to come up with a solution, and the Quarter was sounding a little too quiet.

Permissive drinking laws... For years, two cherished Louisiana traditions have been having a legal drink on your 18th birthday, and getting a daiquiri to go from a drive-thru stand. The drive-thru daiquiri shacks are slowly going the way of the buffalo nickel and the McLean Deluxe, but the young drinking age is struggling to hang on. Although the legal limit was officially raised to 21, a lawsuit has challenged the constitutionality of the new law. Whatever the outcome, nobody really expects the drinking age to stay at 18.

The latest trends... Don't need them. New Orleans prides itself as being a little set off from the rest of the country, and we tend to pick and choose which of the latest crazes we'll adopt. Moshing and tattoos finally arrived, but don't look for poetry slams, raves, scones, or a Starbucks. In this town, yuppies go dancing to accordion music, and hip high school kids play tubas in nightclubs.

the clu

b scene

Your search for real jazz
has led you crawling
through the door of this
street corner juke joint.
Inside, a folding table
buckles under the weight of
a pot of red beans. "Help

yourself," nods the bartender. You fill a paper plate and order a Dixie beer. Sitting at the bar is a row of guys in jeans and T-shirts, all hunched over their own paper plate of beans.

Suddenly, a teenager crashes through the front door; he's hauling two enormous sections of a tuba. As if in some James Cagney movie, your companions at the bar suddenly lift up leather cases, then they snap them open to reveal shiny brass horns. Turn your head, and the joint is packed. The tuba starts blasting like some syncopated steam engine, and trumpets and trombones honk and wheeze in reply.

You made it, you're here; it's New Orleans and this is jazz, and you just can't believe your luck.

Across town, in an even smaller club—this one located behind a bail bond agency—the Soul Queen of New Orleans is teaching her audience how to wave their white table napkins. She sings, "I made my reservation/I'm leaving town tomorrow," but she'll be back here the next night, and the next weekend, too. Meanwhile, over in a bowling alley, a six-and-a-half-foot-tall zydeco player is squeezing the breath from an accordion, while a thin man dancing on a bar nearly slaps his head against the spinning blades of a ceiling fan.

And, in this old cotton warehouse near the river, a shirtless, muscle-bound drummer throws his trap set at a crowd of college students. They assemble it just in time for the drummer to leap at them and start pounding the skins. Just up the street, suited dancers strut under spotted disco lights and floating bouquets of purple balloons, as if suspended in an eternal prom night. While in the back of a smoky bar in the Uptown neighborhood, a blues guitar player wraps duct tape around his hands and mutters something about blisters.

These scenes repeat every night, each week, month after month. New Orleans is the cradle of jazz, the city of the second line, the place where music spills from doorways and circles the block. Some towns, they talk about a pace of life; others are said to have a pulse. New Orleans has a tempo.

And that tempo isn't always only jazz. Zydeco, Latin, reggae, even klezmer music, can be found without much trouble, and the rock scene is booming enough that some optimists claim New Orleans is the next Seattle. (Yeah, yeah, sure.) Traditional sounds have dominated the aural landscape so long that even a touring New Orleans punk band will usually face down at least one request to play "Iko Iko." But recent developments have expanded the scope of New Orleans rock, and a number of Big Easy acts are being snatched up by major labels. No identifiable New Orleans rock sound has yet emerged, but among its brighter stars are: glam-rocker James Hall; popsters Better Than Ezra and Deadeye Dick; and roots rockers Cowboy Mouth, the Continental Drifters, Iguanas, Anders Osborne, and the subdudes. The local presence of a couple of well-regarded recording studios—especially Daniel Lanois' Kingsway—ensures that the local scene is frequently energized by visiting rockers in town to record and hang out for a while. A number of rock icons, including Alex Chilton, reside here, and there are many artists—Bob Dylan among them—who may or may not own a house in the city, depending on which rumor you choose to believe.

There is much to do in the French Quarter, but there is also much to enjoy off the beaten track. New Orleans is a city of distinct *faubourgs* (neighborhoods). The funky Faubourg Marigny is just across Esplanade Avenue from the French Quarter. Treme, home to several tiny, down-home jazz bars, is on the other side of Rampart Street. The Garden District, Uptown, and Carrollton are just a pleasant streetcar ride from downtown. Mid-City requires an easy cab ride or a ride on the Canal Street bus, which is somewhat daunting to board, if only because the destination sign reads "Cemeteries."

Getting Past the Velvet Rope

What velvet cord? Don't look for gatekeepers here; New Orleanians—the original slackers—couldn't care less. The longest line at **City Lights** is to park your car; anyone with five bucks and the proper attire will be whisked through the door. Ditto for **Oz** and the **House of Blues**, except for the part about proper attire: at these clubs, anything goes. Live music events at clubs such as **Mid-City Lanes** and the **Howlin' Wolf** may have long lines, especially during Mardi Gras and Jazz Fest. Here's a local trick: arrive early to pay the cover and get your hand stamped, then go out to eat. When you return to the club, go to the front of the line and show your hand stamp, then walk right in.

The Names To Watch Out For

For New Orleans music fans, the usual question isn't where to go, it's what bands to see. Locals tend to say things like, "I'll see you at the Iguanas" or "Are you going to be at Kermit tonight?" And for good reason: this is a city replete with live music talent. It's always a treat to catch local marquee names such as **Wynton Marsalis**, **Harry Connick, Jr.**, the **Neville**

Brothers, the **Radiators**, and the **subdudes** when they play on (or return to) their home turf. But scores of other performers are also household names in New Orleans, and they give frequent shows at various venues around town. It's a good bet that at least a few of these acts will be in town on any given weekend. **Kermit Ruffins** first gained local fame as the lead singer and trumpet player for the **Rebirth Brass Band**. His current group, the **Barbecue Swingers**, plays traditional jazz and swing, with a title that reflects Ruffins' habit of cooking barbecue at his gigs. His trumpet, high-grade sandpaper voice, and convivial stage presence are often compared to that of a young Louis Armstrong. Satchmo's songs are part of Ruffins' repertoire, along with happy tunes about getting loaded, such as the old jazz homage to cannabis, "When You're a Viper," and an original, "I'll Drink Ta Dat." Catch the "big boss with the hot sauce" at Donna's, Vaughan's, and dozens of other locations around town. If **Leigh "Li'l Queenie" Harris** never sings another note in her life, she'll be beloved in this town for her song "My Darlin' New Orleans," a peppy anthem to streetcars, dancing on beer kegs, and oyster-flavored kisses. Early in her career, Queenie's passionate vocals earned her comparisons to Janis Joplin, but her range, style, and choice of music can't be easily pigeonholed. Her latest project has been fronting a virtuoso string band called **Mixed Knots**, which plays memorable versions of anything from bluegrass to Prince. Catch Li'l Queenie at the Mermaid Lounge and Carrollton Station, among other clubs. **Peter Holsapple** is a relatively new addition to the New Orleans scene. He arrived in town in the early '90s, and has had a big presence both as a solo artist and member of the roots rock band **Continental Drifters** (though he may be better known around the country as a former member of the punk–pop band the dBs, as well as for his tours with R.E.M. and Hootie & the Blowfish). Holsapple often hosts an acoustic mike night at the Carrollton Station; look for his honey–voiced wife and Drifter bandmate Susan Cowsill (yes, of that Cowsill family) to join him on stage for unforgettable duets. Look for the Drifters to play the Howlin' Wolf.

The New Orleans Gambit Weekly newspaper calls the **Soul Rebels** "the bad boys of brass band music." They play their tubas, saxophones, and trumpets while attired in combat fatigues, but their original rap/brass/reggae songs such as "Let Your Mind Be Free" are upbeat, positive-message tunes. They have a big following among local brass-band fans, and their shows at clubs such as Donna's always draw a crowd. The latest in a long line of New Orleans piano wizards—among whom have been Professor Longhair and James Booker—is **Davell Crawford**. A grandson of the legendary R&B artist James "Sugarboy" Crawford, Davell (he frequently performs under one name) can pump the traditional New Orleans piano with the best of them. Hear him anywhere from Tipitina's to Snug Harbor, or if you're really lucky, you can catch him leading a full gospel choir at the House of Blues on Sunday. **Jason Marsalis** is the youngest of a seemingly endless line of musical Marsalises, which has included his big brothers Wynton and Branford. Still in college, Jason is already a prodigious drummer, and his shows attract the best players in town, who either play in the band or sit in for a few songs. He can be heard at just about any real jazz club in the city, especially Snug Harbor and Funky Butt. In 1996, the jazz scene was energized by the return of trumpeter and composer **Terence Blanchard**, who moved back to town from New York. A Columbia recording artist, Blanchard is an adventurous stylist who introduces new elements into his work (including his 1996 recorded collaboration with Brazilian vocalist Ivan Lins), and he's best known for his scores to many of Spike Lee's recent films. Look for Blanchard to play the New Showcase Lounge. When jazz trumpeter **Nicholas Payton** was four years old, his dad (local musician Walter Payton) bought him a trombone kazoo at the Jazz Fest, and he went on stage with the Young Tuxedo Brass Band. Now in his twenties, the young Payton is making his own records on the Verve label, and appeared as Oran "Hot Lips" Page in the 1996 Robert Altman film *Kansas City*. He also frequently hits the local jazz club circuit; look for his name at Snug Harbor.

Among local rock bands, **Dash Rip Rock** and **Cowboy Mouth** put on the best shows. Dash is a longstanding local institution, playing straight-up, barroom rock & roll for crowds that include old fans and young college students. Members of the group are full of stage antics, and guitarist Bill Davis is not above a few Vegas-Elvis moves as the night wears on. Cowboy Mouth benefits from its roster of charismatic members, each of whom could (and frequently does) lead his own band. The songs range from smashing country-rock to brooding singer-songwriter, but the Mouth is best known for the theatrical improvisations of drummer Fred LeBlanc, who has been known to throw his drums into the crowd, climb the scaffolding at Jazz Fest, and tight-rope across club rafters. Audience members will be expected to lie on the floor and jump up in unison at least once each show. This is the band most in demand among local college students; catch both Dash and the Mouth at Tipitina's, the Rendon Inn, and the Howlin' Wolf.

Joe Clay may be one of the most unique comeback stories in rock 'n' roll history. He made a couple hits in the 1950s and even appeared on the "Louisiana Hayride" with Elvis. But thirty years later, he was working as a bus driver in Gretna (a small town across the river from New Orleans) when he received a call in the middle of the night. On the line was a promoter in England, who was calling Clay to let him know that his old sides were charting again in England. A great drummer with clear, teen-aged, Buddy Holly-like vocals, Clay now plays around town with the Clements brothers; look for them at Mid-City Lanes. For years, one of New Orleans' buried musical treasures has been bluesman **Walter "Wolfman" Washington**'s Saturday shows at the Maple Leaf. He's a magnificent vocalist and guitarist, whether he's playing gut-stabbing blues or dancable R&B. Slow-dancing to a Wolfman ballad is the surest way to get a first date off to the right start. Finally, a number of performers from South Louisiana perform regularly in town. **Boozoo Chavis** and **Beau Jocque** are two of the best zydeco players. Chavis is a living legend who recorded the first zydeco single in the mid-1950s, "Paper in My Shoe." He's still a dynamic performer, usually dressed in a Stetson hat and a plastic apron (to protect his accordion). Beau Jocque is a younger player who mixes zydeco, rap, and classic rock; *Rolling Stone* magazine likened his unique sound to a shotgun wedding between Clifton Chenier and ZZ Top, officiated by John Lee Hooker. Both players can be heard at the Mid-City Lanes. When they perform shows together during Jazz Fest, the crowds are some of the biggest in town. Also from the country is the young "swamp rocker" **C.C. Adcock**. His style blends rockabilly and classic swamp pop with a restless punk sensibility, and his sweaty shows at the Mermaid Lounge are cited in local papers in annual "top ten" lists. At the other end of the age spectrum lie the eightysomething Cajun players in the **Hackberry Ramblers**, who also frequently perform the Mermaid for an enthusiastic crowd with a median age of about one-fourth that of the band's oldest member. There's nothing like seeing a bunch of slackers and punkers in their twenties dancing around to the Ramblers, who are always attired in cowboy hats, suspenders, and bolos. Don't miss it.

French Quarter Clubs

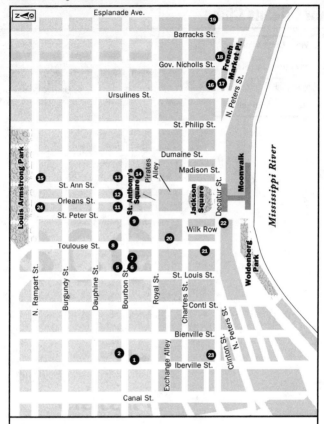

Big Daddy's Lounge **7**

Cajun Cabin **5**

Cat's Meow **11**

Chris Owens Club **6**

The Crystal **16**

Donna's Bar & Grill **15**

Fritzel's European Jazz Club **12**

Funky Butt **24**

The Gold Club **1**

House of Blues **23**

Jimmy Buffett's
 Margaritaville Cafe **17**

Maiden Voyage **2**

Maxwell's Toulouse
 Cabaret **20**

The Mint **19**

O'Flaherty's Irish
 Channel Pub **21**

Oz **14**

Palm Court Jazz Cafe **18**

Parade **13**

Preservation Hall **9**

River Rats **8**

Steamboat Natchez **22**

New Orleans Clubs

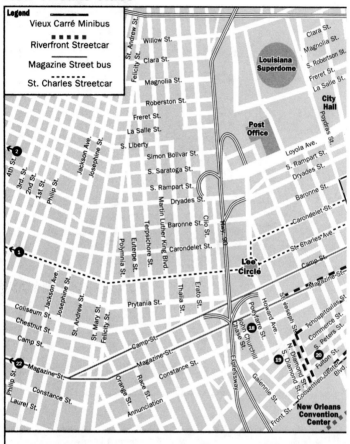

Legend
- Vieux Carré Minibus
- Riverfront Streetcar
- Magazine Street bus
- St. Charles Streetcar

Cafe Brasil **12**	Flamingo Casino New Orleans **17**
Callahan's **7**	Howlin' Wolf **20**
Carrollton Station **1**	Jefferson Orleans North **7**
Check Point Charlie's **9**	Jimmy's Music Club & Patio Bar **1**
Cima Super Club **7**	Madigan's **1**
City Lights **19**	The Lion's Den **5**
Club Whispers **7**	The Maple Leaf **1**

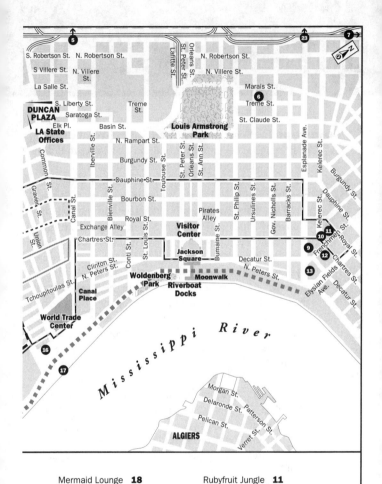

Mermaid Lounge **18**
Mid-City Lanes **5**
The Neutral Ground
  Coffee House **2**
New Showcase Lounge **23**
Pete Fountain's **16**
Rendon Inn **1**

Rubyfruit Jungle **11**
Señor Phroggs **7**
Siam Cafe **13**
Snug Harbor **10**
Tipitina's **22**
Trasure Chest Casino **7**
Treme Music Hall **6**

Overhyped... When Jerry Lee Lewis first played the House of Blues, the veteran rock 'n' roller took a look around at his seven-million-dollar surroundings and mused, "They call this the House of Blues?" The Killer then went on to recall the real blues houses of his early career.

Jerry Lee got it right. Whatever its pluses, the **House of Blues** suffers from a slick style and attitude that just doesn't fit its name. On first entry, intrepid visitors find themselves surrounded by security guards wearing headsets. A greeter at the street quickly asks, "Dinner or show?" then directs them to stand in the first line until they're ushered to the will-call window or through the front door, after which they pass another table of H.O.B. staff to enter the club. This may not sound unusual by New York club etiquette, but it sure ain't the way people like to do things in *this* town. This is one reason why locals have tagged this place "The House of Rules."

Certainly, the joint has its attractions. It's as climate-controlled as a shopping mall. The sound and lights are state-of-the-art. Many recent shows—including appearances by Bob Dylan and Eric Clapton—have offered rare opportunities to see superstars up close; others have given local heroes, like bluesman John Mooney and trumpeter Kermit Ruffins, the chance to strut their stuff on a big stage—and Mooney even recorded an excellent record on the fledgling House of Blues label. Even those who grumble the loudest about H.O.B. have to admit it has a superior calendar of musical events.

Owned by a collection of rock veterans and movie stars, and decorated in folk art and CD-ROM programs played on suspended monitors, the House of Blues may pay sincere tribute to all the great musicians who cut their teeth in the juke joints of the South; but there's little point in tributes when real blues houses can still be found all around New Orleans. So who goes to the House of Blues? Judging from their disinterest in the music, much of the crowd seems to have wandered here from the Hard Rock Cafe, looking for the next scene. On more than one occasion, a rude, talking audience has nearly drowned out the live performers, especially during low-key, acoustic shows. Music fans be warned: a show at this house may just give you the case of the blues.

Even more overhyped... Bourbon Street is actually named for the old French ruling family and not the liquor, but there's no two ways about it: this tourist trap goes down like a big, bar-brand, watered-down, rotgut cocktail. Neither an inferno of sin nor a treasure trove of great jazz, Bourbon Street—at least the most-trafficked blocks closest to Canal Street—has more in common with other ticky-tacky vacation spots, like the Wisconsin Dells and Gatlinburg, Tennessee, than it does with a real music strip. Let's start with the rock clubs: most of the bands that proffer their Led Zep covers here can't find work at any other club in town. Then there's the ubiquitous karaoke at **Cat's Meow** and **River Rats**, where would-be rock stars have their vocals turned so far down in the mix that they are barely audible. The result: just another bad dance club. As you stroll the rest of the strip, you're mostly looking at lame dance clubs, garish souvenir marts, and overpriced restaurants.

The exceptions? The few talented performers to be found here include bluesman Bryan Lee at the **Old Absinthe House Bar** (see The Bar Scene), Cajun rockers Mamou at **Cajun Cabin**, and trumpet legend Al Hirt at **Chris Owens Club**. Still, even these musicians must contend with less-than-hip crowds who expect to hear a simple-simon collection of standards and greatest hits. The best strategy is to give the first few blocks of Bourbon Street a once-over, and then keep walking up the street— to either **Fritzel's European Jazz Club**, that hot pair of happening dance clubs **Oz** and **Parade**, or the Faubourg Marigny neighborhood, located across Esplanade Avenue.

See-and-be-scenes... If New Orleans has a Greenwich Village, it's centered around the corner of Frenchmen and Chartres Streets in the Faubourg Marigny. In the span of a

NEW ORLEANS ◟ THE CLUB SCENE

few blocks are some of the town's liveliest clubs: the eclectic music club **Cafe Brasil**, the down 'n' dirty rock club **Check Point Charlie's**, the dance-happy woman's bar **Rubyfruit Jungle**, the top-notch jazz club **Snug Harbor**, and the **Siam Cafe**, which has a winning combination of music and Thai food. Lining the sidewalk are tables that are most often occupied by skinny guys in goatees, while "gutter punks" with nose rings and pierced tongues wander the block, bumming for change or selling videotapes. Often, the street crowd outnumbers the paid customers inside the clubs, and for good reason: the music usually spills through the doors into the street. The corner rocks the hardest during festival season, and this is an especially popular spot for locals to congregate at Mardi Gras.

Another favorite streetside scene is at **The Maple Leaf Club**. Nothing but a single glass door separates Oak Street from the stage of this Uptown nightclub, and that door is usually left open during the summer months. The result: a sidewalk of dancers, especially for Cajun and zydeco shows.

Where to pretend you're a Cajun... A few downtown Cajun restaurants feature live music; while the bands can be among the best, the scene isn't too popular with locals. A better option is Sunday evenings Uptown at **Tipitina's**, where couples two-step and two-time their way around the big dance floor. At this local institution for all kinds of live music, accordionist Bruce Daigrepont leads a live Cajun band on Sundays, and free red beans and rice are served at set break. Sure, Cajun dancers have all kinds of little rules (such as waltzing only in a clockwise circle), but if you stand on the edge of the dance floor with an eager look, you'll probably be offered a friendly lesson. Since all the dancing is done in pairs, this event also functions as a low-key singles scene, especially for thirtysomethings and older. Dress is casual and functional: the only accessory de rigueur is a bandanna.

For the zydeco-dependent... In the mid 1990s, much of the Cajun music fad has shifted to zydeco, and the various Cajun venues around town have lost much of their crowd to **Mid-City Lanes**' very popular zydeco nights on Wednesdays and Thursdays. Incorporating more blues and R&B in its mix than Cajun music, zydeco is performed by a number of French Creole bands—look for Beau Jocque or the legendary Boozoo Chavis—who drive in each week from western Louisiana to perform on accordion and a corrugated metal "scrubboard." Compared to Cajun, the dancing is more burly and less twirly, and the crowd is more racially mixed and a little younger than what you'll find at Tip's. By the way, Mid-City Lanes is, strictly speaking, a bowling alley (in Mid-City, naturally), but the heaving dance floor discourages tournament play, to say the least. Zydeco bands also play Uptown at the pretty **Maple Leaf Club**, which recently installed a new cherry oak dance floor (much easier on the ankles than the previous concrete). Look for Rockin' Dopsie, Jr. to play on Friday nights, and occasional bands on Sundays.

What a second line is and where to do it... Call it the wave, New Orleans–style. The second line is a dance most frequently done outdoors, with much waving of white handkerchiefs and hoisting of umbrellas to local classic tunes like "Hey Pocky Way" and "Iko Iko." Singer Irma Thomas likes to say that people in this town will second-line to celebrate just about anything, from a good batch of gumbo to finding out that the pregnancy test came back negative. Thomas' own club, **The Lion's Den**, is the best place to second line indoors—when she performs, Thomas even passes out little embossed white napkins. (Please, no umbrellas indoors. They're just as unlucky here as in the rest of the country.) The Lion's Den crowd varies nightly: sometimes it's all locals, other nights it's hip out-of-town fans.

The forecast calls for spontaneous second lines whenever a brass band is playing at **Donna's Bar & Grill**, a barbecue joint on the fringe of the French Quarter, or at **Treme Music Hall** out in Treme. Both draw a younger than the Lion's Den. Here you'll see a skillful hybrid of second-line and break dancing; it's all very fast and furious, and sometimes competitive. For the adventurous, these are also good places to learn about other brass band clubs, second-line parades, and even Mardi Gras Indian events, many of which are only advertised by word-of-mouth or hand-distributed announcements. Second lines are also popular at music festivals. The most tried-and-true way to find a second line, however, is to be at the right street corner at the right time, and let it find you.

Where to hear traditional jazz in the French Quarter...

Most people who visit New Orleans manage at least a glimpse through the smoky glass windows of tiny **Preservation Hall**, if only because the jazz club is located next to Pat O'Brien's. (By the way, those special windows were installed for the filming of a Steve McQueen movie.) For some, this is a rustic, uncompromising music club that's the highlight of a trip to New Orleans; to others, it's the worst kind of tourist trap, with a long line, short music sets, no bar, narrow, wooden benches, and dilapidated mason-board walls. Still, even locals who won't fight the crowds to come here have a special affection for the Hall: before it opened, many of the jazz greats like Sweet Emma, Kid Thomas, and the Humphrey Brothers had nowhere else to play. A lot of these older players have since passed on, but this is still the surest place to hear the vintage sounds: think of it as a living history museum of jazz. And if that guy in the salmon shorts drops his camera on your head while he claps to "When The Saints Go Marchin' In," it helps to remember that it only cost three bucks to get in. Expect a long line, especially on weekends. Some survival tips: despite what it may seem, you don't have to leave when the set is over—take a seat near the far wall, keep your position, and just let everybody jostle around you. Also, the Hall may not have its own bar, but you can always bring drinks in with you.

Some of the same bands who play Preservation Hall also perform in the more ornate **Palm Court Jazz Cafe**. This French Quarter Creole restaurant was immortalized in a song by jazzman Danny Barker—the chorus of the tune goes "Palm Court Strut, swing your butt," but there's really not much butt swinging or any other dancing here. Instead, Palm Court offers traditional New Orleans jazz in a fashionable cafe with tile floors, white tablecloths, and gleaming ceiling fans. You'll be charged a cover to sit at the tables; locals often take a stool at the bar, where it's free. (You'll probably be sitting side-by-side with local jazz musicians.)

Located right in the middle of a busy Bourbon Street block, **Fritzel's European Jazz Pub** is as multicultural as jazz itself, run by a German (named "Dutch") as a home for European jazz players. The fine clarinetist, Jack Maheu, hosts the lively weekend show, a late-night magnet for players working the Quarter. Expect some obscure jazz tunes: these are guys who want to kick back a bit and play something besides "Saints." And finally, the **Steamboat Natchez** offers a real Mississippi River experience: an early-evening, two-hour jazz dinner cruise that features the excellent Dukes of Dixieland band. The music is great, the food OK, but the scene is strictly for tourists.

Where to hear contemporary jazz... Writing in the *New York Times*, jazz critic Tom Piazza opined, "In New Orleans, which is once again a hotbed of talent second only to New York, an amazing group of players is centered around the nightclub Snug Harbor." Indisputably the town's chief club for contemporary jazz (albeit styles that are still firmly grounded in tradition), **Snug Harbor** offers frequent performances by pianist and jazz patriarch Ellis Marsalis, whose progeny includes trumpeter Wynton (currently with Lincoln Center in New York), Branford (late of "The Tonight Show"), and other active musical sons. This Faubourg Marigny club is also the home court of young jazz lions of repute, such as trumpeter Nicholas Payton. Tickets are a little higher here than at other music clubs in town, but many of these shows would fetch twice the price—or more—in other cities. Don't expect creature comforts: the Snug is snug, with small tables set close together. The crowd is generally upscale, well-dressed, very knowledgable about jazz, and attentive to the action onstage. You can order food from the kitchen (the restaurant is known for its big burgers and loaded baked potatoes), but if you try to munch on a sandwich during Miles Davis' "So What," expect to receive some real nasty glares from the jazzies at the other tables.

The hot new clubs for hot jazz... In 1996, the local renaissance in funky jazz clubs included the addition of one new club, and the expansion of an old favorite. As more and more young players are starting to migrate to New Orleans (in a large part due to the strong jazz programs at local universities), the jam sessions and scheduled shows at these clubs keep getting hotter, and closing time keeps getting later. **Funky Butt** opened to rave reviews during Jazz Fest season and immediately began attracting the new crop of local jazz artists. The interior is designed like an old Storyville bordello: a giant painting of a nude woman greets visitors in the downstairs restaurant (see Late Night Dining). The upstairs Danny Barker Room is named for a beloved banjo player, storyteller, and friend of Richard Rochester, the club owner. Barker died in the mid-'90s, and his tribute room is painted in deep red hues and finished in gold plate and art deco–style etched glass. "It's as far from Planet Hollywood as it's possible to be and still be in the French Quarter," Rochester once told the *Times-Picayune*. Funky Butt is located on Rampart Street, on the edge of the Quarter and across the street from Armstrong Park. Harder to reach is the **New Showcase Lounge**, a neighborhood club located on Broad Street, in the residential Gentilly neighborhood. Opened in 1993 by a pair of brothers (who are both pharmacists by day), the Showcase started a regular music schedule in 1995, with live jazz Tuesday through Thursday, and on Saturday and Sunday. The atmosphere is a blend of formal and casual that's unique to local jazz dens. The decor consists of red tablecloths, ceiling fans, a few Christmas-style ornaments, and bare light bulbs. Patrons may arrive dressed in shirt sleeves or suits, while musicians are usually attired in white shirts and tie. Much of the Showcase crowd is composed of local jazz players, and the Gentilly location is off the beaten track, which keeps the action fairly hidden from most locals and nearly all tourists. But it's gaining prominence: local Atlantic recording artists Henry Butler and Wess Anderson held record release parties here in 1996, and WWOZ-FM broadcasts a show here each month. If you're looking for great music and an inviting local scene, it's well worth the drive or cab ride over here.

Where the rock rolls... By far the most consistent, progressive, high-quality rock venue is downtown in the Warehouse District. The **Howlin' Wolf** presents both local and touring artists in a dark, warehouse-like room that features heavy wooden beams, a concrete floor, and a new second level. The club owner seems to have an uncanny intuition about which artists are about to break on the national scene—acts such as Alanis Morissette play the Wolf just months before they return to town to fill the Lakeside Arena. Tulane University's campus radio station, WTUL, also sponsors frequent shows here.

Bands that are up-and-coming (or at least trying to be) play **Check Point Charlie's**, a gritty, no-cover bar/paperback library/laundromat at the border between the French Quarter and the Faubourg Marigny. Expect loud sounds that range from hardcore to funk to the blues, all played for a crowd that, as the night progresses, may become too blitzed to tell the difference.

Look for local rock on the schedules of other venues—such as the tiny **Mermaid Lounge** in the Warehouse District, along with larger houses like the **Rendon Inn** in Uptown, the **House of Blues** in the Quarter, and Uptown's dark and grungy **Jimmy's**. Once the standard bearer of traditional New Orleans sounds, **Tipitina's** now throws local and national rock acts into the mix—and there's nothing quite like seeing Cowboy Mouth's drummer/performance artist high-wire it across this celebrated Uptown club's second-story rafters.

Where to lose your blues... New Orleans doesn't really claim its own distinct shade of the blues, à la Chicago, Kansas City, or the Mississippi Delta—you can hear everything from traditional acoustic Delta to bottom-heavy Chicago electric, though few venues present an exclusive roster of blues (despite its name, the **House of Blues** offers an eclectic mix of everything from bluegrass to alternative). You can get the surest shot of blues night after night right on Bourbon Street, at the **Old Absinthe House Bar** (see The Bar Scene), where the house band is Bryan Lee and the Jump Street Five. Originally from Two Rivers, Wisconsin, Lee is an accomplished guitarist and singer who wins much acclaim on his international tours. Unfortunately, his local gigs occasionally suffer from too many chestnuts that he feels obliged to roast up for this Bourbon Street crowd. But if you sit in front and shout out a request for a tune like Elmore James' "You Been So Mean To Me," or for one of Lee's own fine compositions, you'll be richly rewarded.

The town's best buried blues treasure is John Mooney's Sunday night gig at **Madigan's** in Uptown. Mooney combines Son House guitar work with second-

NEW ORLEANS ◡ THE CLUB SCENE

line rhythms, all refracted through his own feverish personality. Lately, he's been getting the recognition that's been long overdue, and his solo gigs at this small bar may become an endangered species.

Other artists to keep your ears on include Snooks "the Human Jukebox" Eaglin, a classic blues and R&B guitarist who's recorded with Professor Longhair; he frequently performs at the **Mid-City Lanes** in Mid-City, and at the **Howlin' Wolf** in the Warehouse District. A notorious local character, J. Monque'D—a great harpist and vocalist who purveys classic sounds from Howlin' Wolf to Muddy Waters—does frequent stints at **Mid-City Lanes** and various venues around town. Relative newcomer Corey Harris, who paid his dues playing street music in the French Quarter, pours out raw, acoustic-style Delta blues, and his star is rapidly ascending; if you're lucky, you might catch him at the **Mermaid Lounge**, in the Warehouse District. Downtown at **Vic's Kangaroo Cafe** (see The Bar Scene), the gentleman harpist Rockin' Jake exhibits a showman's flair as he leads a blues ensemble through a night of covers and originals. And it's a bit of a drive, but on weekends a lively, college-age dance crowd descends on the memorable **Rivershack Tavern** out in Jefferson (see The Bar Scene) for roadhouse-style blues.

Life's a drag... If you're looking for your own personal *Crying Game,* New Orleans offers plenty of options. Female impersonation has a long and distinguished tradition in this city, dating back to the freewheeling days of Storyville's turn-of-the-century lavish burlesques. Each Mardi Gras, the "Bourbon Street Awards" is one of the nation's best gay fashion shows, with the topmost frills and feathers of many costumes reaching second-story balconies. Drag shows here run the gamut from sleazy "boys-will-be-girls" bars on Bourbon Street to the bawdy-yet-tasteful cabaret of **The Mint**. Named for the old U.S. Mint located right across Decatur Street, this former jewelry store in the Faubourg Marigny has a classic New Orleans look, with pressed tin, ceramic tile floors, and sprays of fresh lilies. Each Saturday at 11pm the "Profiles" show presents a trio of lavishly dressed female impersonators lip-synching to hit songs by a variety of female stars. The enthusiastic crowd is an even mix of locals and tourists, and gays and straights.

Every night is an informal drag show at **Lucky Cheng's** (see The Bar Scene), a restaurant that tests the limits of affirmative action by hiring only Asian–American transvestites as servers. Cheng's stages a full-scale drag show on Mondays at 9pm. On the last Saturday of each month, **Charlene's** (see The Bar Scene) hosts "Viva Las Vamps" for its predominantly lesbian clientele. And on Bourbon Street, Wednesday nights at the frenetic dance club **Oz** are given over to "drag races," where three audience volunteers compete to see who can accomplish the speediest gender transformations.

Dance clubs... Thanks to the vibrant live music scene and a we-don't-care-what's-hot-in-New-York attitude, this city has few dance clubs; young spenders opt instead to go see the Nevilles at the **House of Blues**, or just go out to eat. Among the exceptions: in a spacious old warehouse downtown on the flip side of a marine and manufacturing company is the city's biggest dance club, **City Lights**. A local crowd comes here; it's one of the few places that can convince suburbanites to come into the city on the weekend. The scene is moderately upscale: a few stretch limos are usually sprinkled in the long line of up-market cars waiting for valet parking. Inside, young professionals are packed swivelling-hip-to-swivelling-hip on a multi-tier dance floor, while tuxedoed gents spin a variety of house and high-energy hits. The decor is a blend of low- and high-tech, with balloons, confetti, strobes, and spotlights. A dress code is enforced: women tend toward tight designer dresses, men usually stay with office-style white shirts and ties. This is by far the city's biggest meat market, and there are plenty of second- and third-floor observation posts to check out the goods (City Lights may just be the most heterosexual dance club in the country).

Although **Oz** and **Parade** are somewhat smaller clubs, the dancing here is hotter than at City Lights. Located on opposite sides of Bourbon Street, these are the liveliest gay clubs in town. Oz's welcoming attitude, spirited dance floor, and classic French Quarter decor attracts straights as well (personal ads in New Orleans read, "I enjoy Oz, walks along the river...."), while Parade's crowd is more exclusively gay (although this distinction is beginning to change). Boasting an excellent sound and light system, Oz was rated a top dance club by

NEW ORLEANS ⟨ THE CLUB SCENE

Details magazine in 1994, but a 1995 *Gambit* readers' poll voted Parade the city's best dance club—Parade does have a larger dance floor. On weekends, the crowd weaves back and forth between the two; Tuesday nights at Oz are for all-retro "Dangerous Disco."

A young crowd assembles late at the **House of Blues**, which makes use of its state-of-the-art sound and light systems to transform itself into a popular after-hours dance club when the scheduled live bands are through playing; some nights, more locals show up for the dance scene than for the live music. Thursday's "Heaven Night" is marketed to the gay crowd, and features one of New Orleans' most popular deejays, Mary Pappas.

Another good bet is the cozy dance floor at **Ruby-fruit Jungle**, a women's bar that's popular with gay and straight women and men; the ambiance is all copper, concrete, and chrome. The friendly crowd is local and young, including many twentysomething residents of the surrounding Faubourg Marigny neighborhood. The youngest crowd of all flocks to the smoky, mirrored **Crystal**, which attracts kids from the 'burbs, along with young French Quarter subcultures, such as industrial fans, cyberfreaks, and gutter punks. Nose rings and pierced tongues are big here: if your body hasn't been permanently altered in some way, don't even bother. And the always-crowded **Club Whispers** is especially popular with African-American professionals. Located in New Orleans East, Whispers has nightly specials, such as all-you-can-eat buffets, radio broadcasts, male/female revues, and seafood nights. The crowd of locals is well-dressed and very lively.

Mosh pits to dive into... Like most pop trends, moshing hit New Orleans a few years after it surfaced in the rest of the country, and it still isn't as big as it is in most cities. In recent years, little mosh pits developed for the first time at the "Jazz Fest," for groups like Better Than Ezra. But the local band with the brawniest, most muscular, most moshable sound is Cowboy Mouth—and they explicitly forbid moshing at their shows, and even stop playing when people start slamming. Lack of space prohibits too much action downtown at the **Howlin' Wolf** and Uptown at **Tipitina's**, but there's ample room at the hangarlike **Rendon Inn**

also Uptown (All three clubs charge mosh-friendly general admission.) Larger moshes develop when national touring acts play at the State Palace Theater or the Lakefront Arena (see The Arts).

Where to meet the Latin beat... Caribbean and Latin-American music has always played an important role in the New Orleans sound. You can hear these historical influences in early jazz and in R&B pioneer Professor Longhair's rhumba-inspired piano pounding. Today, a rootsy outfit called the Iguanas is the city's best-loved dance band, and you can often catch the "Iggies" playing a border sweep of swamp pop, Tex-Mex, Mexican, and South American styles for packed houses at any number of clubs, especially **Mid-City Lanes**, **Cafe Brasil**, **The Maple Leaf Club**, and the **Howlin' Wolf**. As indicated by the name, the Faubourg Marigny's Cafe Brasil can be expected to have more Latin bands than most clubs—here's where you might find local dance favorites such as Bob Folse & Fuego, or Mas Mamones. Look for another local favorite, Acoustic Swiftness, purveyors of breezy salsas, bossa novas, and Latin jazz. But for the best merengues and salsas, it's well worth venturing out to the suburb of Metairie to join the local Latin crowd at **Cima Super Club**, which offers the city's best Latin dance band, Los Babies del Merengue, nearly every weekend. The Cima attracts serious dancers from all over the city, including the tiny hamlets located on the other side of the Mississippi River. Many non-Latin music fans haven't yet hipped to the place—but the word is spreading. The scene doesn't really start swinging and swaying until long after midnight, and the band plays until 5am. The lounge atmosphere includes carpeted floors and tables, with a large dance floor and a giant mural of a mountain (the name of the club means "the peak of a mountain"). Attire tends toward suits, dresses, and pumps—but the crowd is here to dance, not show off their sartorial splendors.

Sounds of all nations... Sure, New Orleans's Irish community may not be as big as that in New York or Boston, but it is just as heady with the green beer of enthusiasm. Every year on St. Patrick's Day, a wild parade rolls down Magazine Street through the city's "Irish Channel," with float riders tossing cabbages to onlookers—and occasionally chucking a leafy missile through some unlucky person's second-story apartment window. This spirit is evident every night in the French Quarter at **O'Flaherty's Irish Channel Pub**, home court of musical brothers Patrick and Danny O'Flaherty. This cavernous two-room hall with its handsome 18th-century courtyard boasts great pints of Guiness—the seasoned barkeeps are trained to deliver a slow, masterful draw to guarantee the creamiest head and the best base. For a mixed crowd of locals and tourists, it's the perfect fuel for a night of reeling and jigging. Saturday nights feature Irish dancing, and the O'Flaherty brothers occasionally bring in big-name headliners like Tommy Makem and Paddy Reilly for holidays and special events.

New Orleans also enjoys a sizable reggae community—local favorites include the Shepherd Band, T-Roy & the Vibes, and Cyril Neville and the Uptown All-Stars, whose "second-line reggae" style is a New Orleans original. Look for reggae shows at **Cafe Brasil** in the Faubourg Marigny or Uptown at **Jimmy's**, or take a drive to New Orleans East to catch the Rhythmics scene. Meanwhile, another member of the Nevilles' band, drummer "Mean" Willie Green, provides the beat for the Klezmer All-Stars, a popular Yiddish folk music ensemble with a loyal following (just goes to prove that New Orleanians can cop a groove off of any kind of good dance music). Look for the klezmer crowd at the **Mermaid Lounge** or **Cafe Brasil**.

The tackiest club in town... In the mood to toss back a Jell-O shot and sing the theme song to "The Brady Bunch," while performing an amateur strip show for a birthday girl as your buddies stand around and hoot? Or how about assembling with a room of co-workers and blowing off some steam by doing a chorus-line high-kicking to the tune of "New York, New York"? If so, then **Señor Phroggs** is for you. If not, steer clear. Phroggs, one of the biggest pickup joints for young professionals from Metairie and Kenner, is rarely visited by tourists; in this case, ignorance might be bliss. If you happen to wander by, expect high-energy dance and a nonstop onslaught of retro tunes and sing-alongs, with a heavy dose of old TV theme songs. Occasionally, Phroggs presents live camp, such as the Village People (who turned in a full-costume salute to disco) or KC & the Sunshine Band (whose dismal show featured only KC and a taped backup band). Live or canned, there aren't any sights or sounds that smack of old New Orleans traditions here: Señor Phroggs is entirely a product of American pop culture.

Take it (almost) all off... New Orleans has a reputation as a wild town where pleasure rules, but even on Bourbon Street, strip clubs have their regulations. Despite the promises you'll hear from some doorway barkers, bottomless dancing is prohibited, and performers must perform on a "stage" at least 18 inches off the ground. In recent years, the classic strip club has gentrified and been replaced by the "men's club," a more upscale establishment that prides itself on having classier dancers and classier customers. The most popular of these clubs, **Maiden Voyage**, features an upstairs "Executive Boardroom" complete with a pool table and well-stocked bookshelves (perhaps the silliest touch of all—the books go even more unread than the articles in *Playboy*). Table dances are $20 and are strictly on the up-and-up; touching is kept to a minimum.

Just a half-block off Bourbon, **The Gold Club** is set in a historic building with a long pedigree: formerly the site of the old Playboy Club, a couple centuries earlier it was known as the home of Madame Latrec's Cabaret. (According to "house mom" Kathy Gentry, in the old days Madame Latrec would descend to the stage on a crescent moon, until one fateful night, when a jealous lover shot her in the heart.) This spacious club features the best sound and light system of any strip joint in town, with a musical emphasis on classic seventies and eighties rock. Private dance rooms can be hidden from the world by a pulled curtain. Both the dancers and the clientele here are young and preppy.

The Maiden Voyage and the Gold Club both offer such casino-style amenities as V.I.P. cards and drink specials, along with frequent two-for-one table dances. Don't look for such niceties at **Big Daddy's**. With no cover (but a one-drink minimum), the clientele here is widely varied, and rules are looser; the V.I.P. room is simply a dark corner with a $50 admission ticket. A Bourbon Street landmark for a quarter century, this is the place to find a live boa constrictor languishing beneath a clear plastic stage, a

NEW ORLEANS ⟋ THE CLUB SCENE

shower stall available for use (to wash your favorite dancer), and tape-covered swings suspended from the ceiling. The best strippers here perform with considerable more gusto and skill than the slow-motion, underwater-ballet style popular at the Gold Card and Maiden Voyage. One Big Daddy's stripper named Nisa describes this scene best: "Sometimes I hang from the swing and look down, and I feel like I'm in a Tarantino movie." If you're looking for a vintage, somewhat sleazy, somewhat campy, very "Bourbon Streety" experience, Big Daddy's is your place.

That grand olde country-western thing... Take off those Ropers and that Garth Brooks cowboy hat—you're not going to find too many places to wear them in this town. But if you and your podna just gotta boot-scoot boogie, the best place for you is over at **Boomtown Casino** in nearby Harvey. While the casino boat chugs along the Harvey Canal, the dockside **Boomer Saloon** (see The Bar Scene) presents a variety of recorded and live country acts. Nightly specials include: the "Wild West Talent Rodeo" on Monday; the taping of a live radio show on Tuesday; and live dance lessons on Thursday and Saturday. (Live bands perform on Thursday only.) There are also lots of nightly food specials and a "fun center," where you can drop the kiddies and let them go nuts on the video games.

Other places for country deejay dancing include **Mustang's White Horse Saloon** (formerly Mustang Sally's) out in Kenner, where dance lessons are given Wednesday through Sunday. And for something completely different, the Faubourg Marigny's **Rubyfruit Jungle** offers deejay country line dancing on Tuesday nights in an atypical environment, for a mixed gay and straight clientele. If you're looking for live country bands, check the club listings to see when and where the Swingin' Haymakers or the Wild Peyotes are playing. Both local bands offer a mix of alternative and classic country stylings, and might be playing at venues such as the **Howlin' Wolf** in the Warehouse District, and Uptown at **Carrollton Station**. Also, be sure to check the **Mermaid Lounge** in the Warehouse District to see if those Texas swing/Cajun legends the Hackberry Ramblers are in town.

NEW ORLEANS ⟨ THE CLUB SCENE

Everybody likes to cha-cha-cha... There's really only one place in town to begin the beguine and charge up your cha-cha, and that's **Jefferson Orleans North**. Drowning in a sea of low-rise office buildings, on Wednesdays and Sundays this suburban banquet hall presents ballroom dancing to live big bands. The friendly crowd is 40-plus and attired in suits and dresses, and they certainly know who's leading whom on the tile dance floor. No official lessons are offered, but the big band crowd is always prowling for new proselytes. (This is one of New Orleans' best-kept secrets.)

If you're doing too much tripping when you're tripping the light fantastic, then head out to Metairie where you can hit the parquet dance floor at **Callahan's** for some remedial lessons in cha-cha-cha, West Coast swing, and even that old seventies stand-by, the hustle. Of course, you can spare yourself embarrassment by opting for a somewhat more chic French Quarter spot, **Maxwell's Toulouse Cabaret**, where Harry Connick, Sr. and the Jimmy Maxwell Orchestra hold forth. In a stark, black box theaterlike room, Maxwell's band is fronted by Connick, a capable crooner who just happens to be the District Attorney of New Orleans (but is even better known for his famous son of the same name, who has been known to stop by when in town). Among Maxwell's other choice offerings are Banu Gibson and New Orleans Hot Jazz, a highly recommended outfit that performs jazz obscurities from the twenties and thirties.

Where folks go for folk music... On the stoop outside an unassuming Uptown coffeehouse, a couple of easygoing fellas in shorts and Birkenstocks tune their guitars. Above them, the yellow, red, and blue light falling through a stained-glass window gives you the idea that there's something sacred going down here. The door is open, and the interior is bathed in warm, inviting light. Through the door is **The Neutral Ground Coffee House**, the city's only full-time venue for acoustic singer-songwriters. Named for the grassy bank in the center of New Orleans boulevards (the traditional meeting space for Mardi Gras Indians), the Neutral Ground opened its doors on "tax day" in 1992. Since then, it has kept a busy calendar of about 50 rotating musicians who play for tips from a tiny, back-against-the-wall stage. As is usually par

NEW ORLEANS ✆ **THE CLUB SCENE**

for the course, a few of these players will make you want to beat a hasty retreat to that front stoop. Others, such as Gina Forsyth, Myshkin, and David & Roselyn, are among the city's finest folkies. Look for occasional acts by area rockers who are in the mood to go unplugged, including favorites Anders Osborne and Theresa Andersson. Weekends usually bring the best acts, along with occasional out-of-towners. If you're in a particularly mellow mood and could use a cup of coffee, a piece of cake, and a few choruses of "He Was a Friend of Mine," here's your place.

Sing me a song, piano man... New Orleans has long been a piano town, spawning such legendary figures as Fats Domino, Professor Longhair, Dr. John, and Tuts Washington. Another one of the greats, Eddie Bo, still performs every week in the French Quarter at **Jimmy Buffett's Margaritaville Cafe**. A figure from the golden era of Crescent City R&B, Bo is best remembered for his hit, "Check Mr. Popeye" (named for a dance craze that was especially popular in the New Orleans area). Known for his distinct playing and his ubiquitous turban, Bo's show is a perfect way to start an evening of musical explorations. His no-cover solo act gets under way at 5pm, Thursday through Sunday.

Jazz standards and occasional show tunes emanate from the 1948 Steinway in the back of **Lafitte's Blacksmith Shop** (see The Bar Scene), that romantic French Quarter landmark. Performers include the talented John Gordon, who can either play or fake his way through just about any request. The grand piano at the **Polo Lounge** (see The Bar Scene), downtown in the Windsor Court Hotel, provides the soundtrack for various suits and celebs to unwind with martinis and cigars. For the inspired, the Polo also has the city's smallest dance floor, a little octagonal insert in the center of a plush carpet floor. It's big enough for maybe three couples, if they know one another well.

Big names on their home turf... Some of the city's most nationally renowned talents own their own clubs down here, and it's always a pleasure to catch these folks on their home turf. Clarinetist Pete Fountain is treasured locally as much for his annual "half-fast" Mardi Gras parade as for his distinguished musical career; but his club downtown at the Hilton, **Pete Fountain's**, mainly attracts tourists—especially well-heeled, forty-plus fans who remember Pete's frequent appearances on "The Tonight Show" (with Johnny, not Jay). Old-school classy, with red carpet, red walls, and a distinct checkerboard ceiling, the lounge displays such well-worn memorabilia as Fountain's own gold records and a giant Hirshfeld drawing. His playing is like it's always been, spirited and polished, appealing mostly to those forty-plus fans.

In-the-know fans of New Orleans R&B flock to **The Lion's Den**, the home court of Irma Thomas, the revered Soul Queen of New Orleans. She's here most weekends, performing classics such as "It's Raining," "Breakaway," and "Time Is On My Side." The down-home touches in this tiny, plain club in Mid-City include a free plate of red beans and rice, usually prepared by Thomas herself.

Remember the hit song "Mother-in-Law"? Its singer, Ernie K-Doe, certainly does, and to refresh your sense of recall, he opened his very funky **Mother-in-Law Lounge** recently in 1995 in the Treme neighborhood. The quirky K-Doe may not be as polished a performer as Irma Thomas, but his club is a good bet for R&B fans on a night of New Orleans music-exploring. And while Jimmy Buffett isn't exactly a New Orleans musician, he did play street music here in his early years. When he's in town, he'll probably climb on stage at **Jimmy Buffett's Margaritaville Cafe** in the French Quarter to offer up a few lines about those famous missing salt shakers.

Where visiting big names play... One of the best things about the **House of Blues** is that it occasionally provides opportunities to catch big names in clubby environs; Johnny Cash and Aerosmith are among the stars who have rattled the folk art here in memorable shows. But the best way to catch the stars in the bars is just to be at the right place at the right time. Nothing is better than those rare moments when the big names spontaneously jump up on little stages, and it happens with great frequency in New Orleans: Bruce Springsteen joined the Iguanas at **The Maple Leaf Club** Uptown; the Counting Crows' Adam Duritz hopped up on the stage at **Carrollton Station**, also Uptown; Mick Jagger once shook his groove thing at a second-line parade; and even Bob Hope has crooned a tune with the jazz band at **Preservation Hall**.

Laugh's on you... New Orleans has given television some of its best funnymen, funnywomen, and funnyclaypeople. New Orleans gave "Saturday Night Live" Garrett Morris and even the accident-prone Mr. Bill. Others who have emerged from the Big Easy include sitcom stars Ellen DeGeneres and John Larroquette. But you won't find these performers returning home to play the comedy circuit, because there is none. When rare moments of good comedy do surface, it's usually in the form of satires of local life (to catch the jokes, you'd almost need to have lived here for half your life). One team that appeals to both locals and tourists is Becky Allen and Ricky Graham. Allen calls herself a "female drag queen," and the duo's routines of topical humor and sex jokes can often be caught in the Faubourg Marigny at **The Mint**. Other than that, it can be slim pickings. If you absolutely need a sudden infusion of improv comedy, you can try Mid-City's **Movie Pitchers**, but the talent is inconsistent and the scene is very casual. A few Metairie nightclubs rotate comedy nights into their weekly calendars, including **Callahan's**. But if you're really in the mood to yuk along with the pros, the best advice may be to stay in your hotel room and switch on the Comedy Channel.

Sing-along songs... Sandwiched between the music clubs and strip joints of Bourbon Street—and usually attracting a larger audience than both—are the very popular **Cat's Meow** and **River Rats**. These aren't your father's karaoke bars: don't expect to find anyone staring at a monitor and crooning "Feelings." Instead, these franchises have downplayed the biggest risk of karaoke: bad singing. They pump up the bass and drum, and mix the amateur voices in with the originals. The result? Campy dance clubs that feature a lot of classic and alternative rock, while some loaded guy on the stage attempts some Elvis moves and inaudibly belts out his version of Hootie and the Blowfish's latest. The scenes are virtually interchangeable. The crowd is largely Southern college students: imagine spring break in Fort Lauderdale without the swimsuits.

If all this makes you long for a classic piano bar sing-along, turn off Bourbon Street for **Pat O'Brien's** (see The

Bar Scene), and veer right from the foyer into the giant piano bar. Beer steins line the rafters, and a rowdy crowd of tourists of varying ages fills the tables, where they slosh drinks from side to side and delightedly flub scatological songs like "All day long she sits and swings/All day long she swings and sits/That's Sara, Sara, swingin' on the shed house door." A pair of pianists—usually including the buoyant Jerry Nuccio—keeps things rolling. And if you truly harbor dreams of being discovered singing "Disco Inferno" in a suburban nightclub, check out amateur night at **Callahan's**, out in Metairie, which features their house band backing Barry Gibb wannabes in disco tunes and mid-eighties radio hits.

For teeny-boppers... All-ages shows are another national phenomenon that hasn't really caught on in this town, and for good reason: until recently, every show was pretty much an all-ages show. But enforcement of the drinking age is getting tougher, and recent legal challenges may even threaten to raise it from 18 to 21. In response, area clubs are beginning to experiment with alcohol-free shows, especially for touring acts that enjoy a big teen following. Check out the schedule for **Rendon Inn** or **Jimmy's**; early shows are sometimes all-ages. Young audiences also pop up at rock fests, such as the annual Zephyrfest and an annual outdoor shindig sponsored by Tulane University radio station WTUL.

Gambling... Louisiana is currently embroiled in a love-hate relationship with the world of gambling. A former governor, Edwin "Fast Eddie" Edwards, who was a Vegas high-roller, helped usher in many of the state's gambling options. Today there's a state lottery, a trio of blinking video poker machines in nearly every bar (and large video poker "casinos" in truck stops), numerous riverboat casinos on the state's lakes and rivers, and one giant mess of a half-built bankrupt casino wedged right in the middle of downtown New Orleans. At press time, construction on Harrah's casino—which once promised to be the world's largest gambling den—was stalled, and various factions were attempting to renegotiate terms with the city and state. Meanwhile, a new anti-gambling governor promises to put all gaming choices up to a statewide vote. Stay tuned.

The course of riverboat gambling in the New Orleans area has not proved smooth, either. During the first months of operating, a legal loophole allowed captains to stay docked when weather conditions were deemed too risky to ship out. Being docked, of course, allows for more gamblers to board. When the District Attorney noticed that captains were deeming conditions too risky on a daily basis, he took action. As a result, some casinos closed, and others picked up anchor and headed for better fishing waters.

The selection of slots and table games are pretty standard at the remaining boats. Only one of these—**The Flamingo Casino**—tours the Mississippi River along the downtown and French Quarter, offering non-narrated rides that offer a pretty good late-night view of the city's river banks. The Flamingo docks at the Poydras Street Wharf at the New Orleans Hilton. **The Treasure Chest Casino** docks on Lake Pontchartrain, about a half-hour drive from downtown but very near the airport. Treasure Chest runs a good schedule of live New Orleans music, along with golden-oldies touring acts like the Commodores. Finally, the **Boomtown Casino** sits in the boonies, on the not-very-scenic Harvey Canal on the West Bank. To compensate for its location, Boomtown stakes its identity on live and taped country music dances; and locals come here as much to kick up their heels as to raise their stakes.

The Index

Unless otherwise noted, all clubs are open nightly. If no cover charge is indicated, there is none.

Big Daddy's Lounge. For a quarter-century, a pair of mannequin legs have been kicking outside Big Daddy's windows onto Bourbon Street. At the other end of those legs is a classic seedy strip club.... *Tel 504/581–7167. 522 Bourbon St., French Quarter. 1 drink minimum.*

Boomtown Casino. This riverboat casino compensates for its out-of-the-loop location by offering live country music and dancing.... *Tel 504/366–7711. 4132 Peters Rd., Harvey. Open 24 hours.*

Cafe Brasil. The anchor of a hip street scene in the Faubourg Marigny, this venue offers everything from jazz to Latin to klezmer.... *Tel 504/947–9386. 100 Chartres St., Faubourg Marigny. About $5 cover for live music.*

Cajun Cabin. When the Cajun band Mamou is playing this rowdy bar, the music is good, but the Bourbon Street setting still feels like it's a long distance from the bayous.... *Tel 504/529–4256. 501 Bourbon St., French Quarter. 1 drink minimum.*

Callahan's. This out-of-time Metairie nightclub appeals to the forty-plus local crowd with disco, comedy, and cha-cha-cha—not to mention handy cologne machines in the men's room.... *Tel 504/888–9898. 3213 Kingman St., Metairie.*

Carrollton Station. On weekends, this cozy club is an intimate place to catch local rock and roots music groups—if you're lucky, singer L'il Queenie is on stage.... *Tel 504/865–9190. 8140 Willow St., Uptown. About $5 cover for live music.*

Cat's Meow. Walk in, sign up, choose from hundreds of song options, get onstage, and sing your guts out in this raucous Bourbon Street karaoke dance club.... *Tel 504/523–1157. 701 Bourbon St., French Quarter.*

Check Point Charlie's. Located on the edge of the French Quarter, this dingy rock club features loud music by local up-and-coming blues and rock bands that pass the hat for tips. Plus, there's a 24-hour laundromat in back.... *Tel 504/947–0979. 501 Esplanade Ave., Faubourg Marigny. Open 24 hours.*

Chris Owens Club. Owens' song-and-dance show is a French Quarter institution but locals stay away from her Las Vegas-lite revue. Her club also frequently hosts Grammy-winning trumpet legend Al Hirt.... *Tel 504/523–6400. 500 Bourbon St., French Quarter. $11–$36 cover.*

Cima Super Club. On weekends, Latin dancers from across the city salsa and merengue until early morning at this lively suburban club.... *Tel 504/833–6766. 2726 Causeway Blvd., Metairie. Open late Fri–Sat. $5 cover.*

City Lights. A well-heeled singles crowd flocks to this spacious downtown dance club and meat market, one of the few venues in the city with a dress code.... *Tel 504/568–1700. 310 Howard Ave., Warehouse District. Open Thur–Sun. $5 cover.*

Club Whispers. This very popular dance club in New Orleans East caters to an upscale African-American clientele.... *Tel 504/245–1059. 8700 Lake Forest Blvd., New Orleans East. Cover varies between $5–$10.*

The Crystal. Loud techno music plays for a twentysomething dance crowd dressed in baggy pants and belly shirts that expose the latest navel piercing.... *Tel 504/522–0511. 1135 Decatur St., French Quarter. Open Thur–Sun. $5 cover.*

Donna's Bar & Grill. This laid-back barbecue joint is the stomping grounds for the city's best brass bands. Late-night jazz jam sessions can attract some stellar players.... *Tel 504/ 596–6914. 800 N. Rampart St., French Quarter. Closed Mon. About $3 cover.*

Flamingo Casino New Orleans. This is the most accessible riverboat casino to the Downtown and French Quarter areas, and the cruise offers a nice late-night view of the city…. *Tel 504/587-7777 or 800/587-5825. Poydras Street Wharf at New Orleans Hilton, Downtown. Open 24 hours. $5 admission.*

Fritzel's European Jazz Club. The best place on Bourbon Street to find great traditional jazz, which on weekends plays until the wee hours…. *Tel 504/561-0432. 733 Bourbon St., French Quarter.*

Funky Butt. This new jazz club has late–night jam sessions in a room that's designed like an old New Orleans bordello. Along with Donna's, which is located just a few blocks away, this is one reason why locals are beginning to return to Rampart Street…. *Tel 504/558-0872. 714 N. Rampart St., French Quarter. AE, D, DC not accepted.*

The Gold Club. Part of a regional chain (other locations are in Baton Rouge and Atlanta), this upscale men's club features a large main stage and occasional visits from Penthouse Pets and other adult entertainment celebs…. *Tel 504/524-4354. 727 Iberville St., French Quarter. $3 cover until 7pm, $7 after.*

House of Blues. This $7 million blues joint may seem like a contradiction in terms, but that's what you get when you start with some celebrity investors, then throw in some CD-ROM blues history lessons, an impressive array of local and national bands, and walls and walls of Southern folk art…. *Tel 504/529-1421. 225 Decatur St., French Quarter. $5-$15 cover.*

Howlin' Wolf. Concrete floors, exposed pipes, and massive wood ceiling beams give character to this converted 1850s grain and cotton warehouse, a top venue for alternative rock. Monday is acoustic open mike night…. *Tel 504/523-2551. 828 S. Peters St., Warehouse District. $5-$10 cover.*

Jefferson Orleans North. Each Sunday and Wednesday night, this banquet hall turns into a big band dance club that's popular with the fortysomething and older crowd…. *Tel 504/454-6110. 2600 Edenborn Ave., Metairie. $8 cover.*

THE CLUB SCENE

NEW ORLEANS

Jimmy Buffett's Margaritaville Cafe. Jimmy Buffett's "parrothead" fans meet birds of a feather at this shrine to the singer. Lots of Jimmy photos on the walls, and the man himself does play here when he's in town.... *Tel 504/592–2565. 1104 Decatur St., French Quarter. Music Wed–Sun.*

Jimmy's Music Club & Patio Bar. Rock music in a dark, garage-like club that sits across the street from the streetcar barn.... *Tel 504/861–8200. 8200 Willow St., Uptown. Open Wed–Sun. $5–$10 cover.*

The Lion's Den. This tiny neighborhood bar may not look like a palace, but on weekends it's where you'll find Irma Thomas, the Soul Queen of New Orleans.... *Tel 504/821–3745. 2655 Gravier St., Mid–City. Open Fri–Sat. $5–$15 cover.*

Madigan's. On Sundays, this nondescript neighborhood/college bar turns into one of the town's best-kept music secrets, when blues guitarist John Mooney plays a solo show.... *Tel 504/866–9455. 800 S. Carrollton Ave., Uptown.*

Maiden Voyage. Ads plastered on local taxis and buggies, as well as a prime location on Bourbon Street, make this the best-known strip club in town, a popular destination for visiting businessmen and conventioneers.... *Tel 504/524–0010. 225 Bourbon St., French Quarter. $5 cover until 7:30pm, $10 after.*

The Maple Leaf Club. A lush, canopied back patio; pressed-tin walls and ceiling; a chess table in the front; an attractive new dance floor; and even Sunday poetry readings add to the attraction of this Uptown club booking an eclectic schedule of live music.... *Tel 504/866–9359. 8316 Oak St., Uptown. About $5 cover.*

Maxwell's Toulouse Cabaret. Big band and early jazz in a comfortable setting appeals to a forty-plus crowd.... *Tel 504/523–4207. 615 Toulouse St., French Quarter. Closed Mon. $11 cover.*

Mermaid Lounge. Located under an overpass, this tiny, L-shaped bar is one of the hippest places to hear a variety of bands, ranging from country to punk to surf. You'll probably get lost the first time you try to find it; it's part of the initiation.... *Tel 504/524–4747. 1102 Constance St., Warehouse District. Closed Mon. $5 cover.*

Mid-City Lanes. If you have one night in New Orleans and you want to experience a local music club, this bowling alley is the place to go. Classic Louisiana styles, such as zydeco, New Orleans R&B, and blues, dominate. The crowd likes to dance.... *Tel 504/482–3133. 4133 S. Carrollton Ave., Mid-City. Music Wed–Sat. About $5 cover for live music.*

The Mint. This former jewelry store provides an attractive venue for live music, comedy, and drag shows.... *Tel 504/525–2000. 504 Esplanade Ave., French Quarter. $5 cover.*

Mother-in-Law Lounge. Owned and operated by the irrepressible singer Ernie K-Doe, this funky club presents shows by K-Doe and other R&B artists.... *Tel 504/947–1078. 1500 N. Claiborne St., Treme. Music Sat–Sun. About $5 cover.*

Movie Pitchers. This tiny Mid-City movie theater (named for its liquor license) also hosts live comedy.... *Tel 504/488–8881. 3941 Bienville St., Mid-City. Check listings for comedy show dates. About $5 cover.*

Mustang's White Horse Saloon. Formerly part of the Mustang Sally's chain, this suburban country-western bar has a deejay spinning the latest tunes for light-footed line dancers.... *Tel 504/443–2925. 3406 Williams Blvd., Kenner. Open Wed–Sun. $4 cover.*

The Neutral Ground Coffee House. The soul of the sixties is kept alive in this casual, member-owned co-op, which has music that can be quite good—singer-songwriters, blues, string bands, women's music, and open mike.... *Tel 504/891–3381. 5110 Danneel St., Uptown. Closed Mon. No cover.*

New Showcase Lounge. This friendly neighborhood jazz club is mainly known to local jazz players and buffs, but the music is frequently world–class.... *Tel 504/945–5612. 1915 N. Broad St., Gentilly. $*

O'Flaherty's Irish Channel Pub. Expect a couple of sing-alongs in this friendly Irish bar operated by a pair of musical brothers.... *Tel 504/529–1317. 514 Toulouse St., French Quarter.*

Oz. This very popular Bourbon Street destination features professionals dancing on the bar while amateurs pack the cozy dance floor.... *Tel 504/593–9491. 800 Bourbon St., French Quarter. Closed Mon. $5 cover.*

Palm Court Jazz Cafe. In a Creole restaurant, one of the city's best showcases for traditional jazz.... *Tel 504/525–0200. 1204 Decatur St., French Quarter. Open Wed–Sun. $4 cover for table seats.*

Parade. Upstairs from the Bourbon Pub lies the largest gay disco in town.... *Tel 504/529–2107. 801 Bourbon St., French Quarter. Closed Mon. $5 cover.*

Pete Fountain's. When he's not on tour, the clarinetist toots his own horn at his own club.... *Tel 504/523–4374. New Orleans Hilton Riverside, Poydras at the Mississippi, Downtown. Tues–Sat. $19 cover.*

Preservation Hall. This venerable landmark has a well-deserved reputation for presenting trad jazz in a dilapidated shoebox of a room. Expect no drinks and few creature comforts.... *Tel 504/522–2841. 726 St. Peter St., French Quarter. $3 cover.*

Rendon Inn. When touring alternative rock acts play this hangarlike building, there's a whole lot of moshing going on.... *Tel 504/822–9858. 4501 Eve St., Uptown. Call for live music schedule. Cover varies between $5–$10.*

Rhythmics. Here's the place to take the cap off your dreads and join the city's reggae community.... *Tel 504/241–6100. 7150 Downman Rd., New Orleans East. Music Sat–Sun. $5 cover.*

River Rats. This club absorbs the spillage of crazy karaokers from nearby Cat's Meow, which is part of the same chain.... *Tel 504/523–2788. 441 Bourbon St., French Quarter.*

Rubyfruit Jungle. High-energy dance music and even weekly country line dancing, for a hip crowd of gays and straights....

*Tel 504/947–4000. 640 Frenchmen St., Faubourg
Marigny. Open Tues–Sat. $5 cover.*

Señor Phroggs. A local singles hangout in Metairie, with a mix
of high-energy dance and various goofy promotions.... *Tel
504/834–4010. 3217 Melvil Dewey Dr., Metairie. About
$5 cover.*

Siam Cafe. Upstairs in the Dragon's Den, you can order Thai
food, recline on floor pillows, and hear a wide variety of
good local music.... *Tel 504/949–1750. 435 Esplanade
Ave., Faubourg Marigny. About $5 cover.*

Snug Harbor. The epicenter of contemporary jazz in New
Orleans, this is one of the most vibrant jazz clubs in the
country.... *Tel 504/949–0696. 626 Frenchmen St.,
Faubourg Marigny. $5–$10 cover.*

Steamboat Natchez. Roll on the river with an evening dinner
cruise featuring the top-flight jazz band the Dukes of
Dixieland.... *Tel 504/586–8777. Docks at Jackson
Brewery, French Quarter. $38.75 for cruise and dinner;
$18.75 for cruise only.*

Tipitina's. Once the preeminent home of both traditional New
Orleans music and big-name touring acts, Tip's now
endures stiff competition from the House of Blues. But this
remains a fine and funky club to hear everything from classic R&B to rock to Cajun.... *Tel 504/895–8477. 501
Napoleon Ave., Uptown. Nights vary. About $5–$15 cover.*

Treasure Chest Casino. Out on Lake Pontchartrain, this casino boat presents classic New Orleans pop and R&B acts,
such as Charmaine Neville and Tommy Ridgley.... *Tel 504/
443–8000 or 800/298–0711. 5050 Williams Blvd.,
Kenner. Open 24 hours. Free admission.*

Treme Music Hall. This neighborhood bar attracts a young,
local crowd with regular shows by favorites like the Rebirth
Brass band.... *Tel 504/596–6942. 1601 Ursulines Ave.,
Treme. Call for music schedule. $3–$5 cover.*

the bar

scene 2

The chronicles of the
Crescent City are writ over
its cocktails: Hurricanes,
mint juleps, Sazeracs.
Perhaps it's because of
those long, hot summers
that Tennessee Williams

knew so well, when only nightfall brings sweet breezes of relief. Or maybe it's because the rowdy shipyards and the famed red-light Storyville district of the city's not-so-distant past always provided a steady flow of customers. One thing is sure: in this town's early years, when the Spanish, French, and American flags were traded like business cards, the Southern night never, ever lacked for activity.

As they say in New Orleans, *la plus ça change....* The more things change, the more they stay the same. Sure, yesteryear's bordellos are today's after-work happy hours; pirate Jean Lafitte's former headquarters now serves cocktails by candlelight, and you can get a late-night sandwich in the home they built for Napoleon. The French Quarter sees nine million visitors each year, and sometimes they all seem to be in the same drink line on Bourbon Street. But in a town that still has no last calls or mandatory closing hours, the dark hours inevitably drift into daylight, and for both pirates and poets, businessmen and bohemians, another New Orleans night becomes history.

The Beaten Path

New Orleans bars can be divided into two categories: on Bourbon Street or off Bourbon Street. **Bourbon Street**, as we've said before, is an overhyped wasteland: even Bourbon's decent bars are primarily filled with Southern fraternity brothers, couples from Peoria getting looped on Hurricanes, and a few dispirited European travelers trying in vain to find the city's soul. Off Bourbon Street is where you'll find everyone else. Bars in the **Faubourg Marigny** cater to boho artists, off-duty musicians, and youth adrift. **Uptown** bars see a lot of action from Tulane and Loyola students. **Downtown** and the **Warehouse District** downtown get young professionals. People from the suburbs usually stay there. But these are rough descriptions at best; New Orleans night owls don't habitually flock together. On any given night, you can expect to see businessmen and bums dancing side-by-side atop the same pool table.

What To Order

Some drinks are like Mt. Everest: you take them on because they're there. Vodka in Russia, steins of beer in Germany, and the red, sticky-sweet **Hurricanes** at Pat O'Brien's, which has been in business since 1933. Perhaps the most popular souvenirs of New Orleans are Pat O's 29-ounce crested Hurricane glasses, which gather dust on bookshelves across the world. (Who would ever actually use one of those again?). The standard Hurricane here includes four ounces of rum, ice, and a pre-made liquid Hurricane mix that's also available in gift shops across town; look for bars that use a variety of rums and fresh fruit juices instead of the mix.

To understand the **Sazerac**, you must first understand absinthe. Introduced to New Orleans in 1835 and outlawed across the country in 1914, the bitter, anise-like absinthe is a naturally occurring narcotic that results from the use of worm-wood in the liqueur's aging process. Absinthe is addictive as hell, and in the nineteenth century, it was all the rage in the Big Easy. Today, the two most important remnants of the absinthe craze are the Old Absinthe House Bar on Bourbon Street and the Sazerac cocktail. The Sazerac, it is said, was originally invented as a tasteful absinthe delivery system, so ladies could properly enjoy their neurotoxin. Similar to an Old-Fashioned, the drink acquires its sweet licorice taste from the locally made Herbsaint liqueur. Other ingredients are Peychaud's bitters, rye whiskey, a twist of lemon, and ice. With the flare of a pizza-tosser, the best bartenders spin the glass in the air to coat the inside with the Herbsaint. The drink is shaken or stirred, then strained and served straight-up.

Due to the difficulty of keeping fresh ingredients in stock (such as eggs, mint leaves, and cucumbers), some of New Orleans' best bars don't serve some of the best New Orleans drinks. The **Ramos Gin Fizz** is especially difficult to find—in fact, the Napoleon House recently discontinued the drink, to the disappointment of its many fans. With a sweet, delicate taste and a frothy texture, this gin drink was invented in 1886 by Henry Ramos at his own establishment, the Imperial Cabinet. Served in a highball glass, the Fizz's flavor comes from lemon juice, one drop of vanilla, and two drops of orange flower water, and it's made fluffy by the shaken egg white. The Napoleon House does still serve up another specialty, the **Pimm's Cup**. Served in a tall glass with a slice of cucumber, this British-born cocktail has a light, sweet-sour taste that is a perfect summer coolant. Also tailor-made for the summer is that quintessential Southern libation, the **mint julep**. Every bar stocks bourbon to make juleps, but the secret is finding a bar that keeps a stock of fresh mint leaves.

Etiquette

You have to be 18 years old (or a reasonable facsimile thereof) to walk into a bar in Louisiana. Historically, Louisiana teens have enjoyed one of the lowest drinking ages in the country, as well as relatively lax enforcement of any laws that happened to be on the books. But modern attitudes about youth and drinking are finally winning out over this long-standing local custom. The fate of the drinking age is still up in the air, due to a legal challenge to recent efforts to boost the limit to the national standard of 21, but the tide is turning. Still, if you're under-age and looking to get away with a drink, the law will probably look the other way. The bad news: enforcement can be arbitrary, swift and harsh, and tourists aren't immune to a trip to central lock-up.

Don't worry about closing time—you won't find any here. The other rules are pretty lax as well. If you're sitting at a local bar, it's common to leave your change on the counter to pay for the next drink; it tells the barkeeps that you'll take care of them later. Otherwise, it's best to tip as you go along. In the past, New Orleans has been notoriously loose about enforcing DWI laws, but things are changing, and few police officers see drunk driving as a cute local custom anymore.

French Quarter Bars

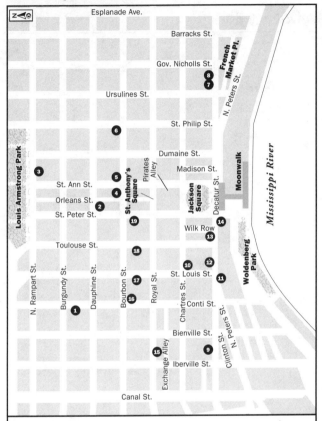

The Bombay Club **1**

Bourbon Pub **5**

Carousel Bar **15**

Crescent City Brewhouse **12**

The Dungeon **18**

Fashion Cafe **13**

Fritzel's European
 Jazz Club **4**

Good Friends **2**

Hard Rock Cafe **11**

House of Blues **9**

Hula Mae's Tropic Wash
 & Beach Cafe **3**

Lafitte's Blacksmith Shop **6**

Lucky Cheng's **17**

Molly's at the Market **7**

Napoleon House
 Bar and Cafe **10**

Old Absinthe House Bar **16**

Pat O'Brien's **19**

Planet Hollywood **14**

Vino! Vino! **8**

New Orleans Bars

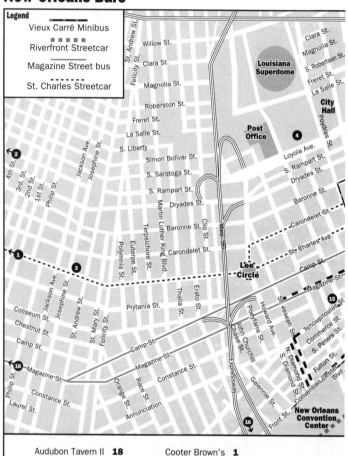

Legend

━━━━ Vieux Carré Minibus

▪ ▪ ▪ ▪ ▪ Riverfront Streetcar

━━━━ Magazine Street bus

- - - - - St. Charles Streetcar

Audubon Tavern II **18**	Cooter Brown's **1**
Bayou Bar **3**	The Daily Planet Espresso Bar **1**
The Boot **1**	Ernst Cafe **14**
Bruno's Bar **1**	F&M Patio Bar **18**
The Bulldog **18**	Hyttops **4**
Carrollton Station **1**	Le Bon Temps Roule **18**
Charlene's **11**	Lucy's Retired Surfers' Bar **15**
Check Point Charlie's **9**	Mid-City Lanes **5**
Columns Hotel **1**	My Father's Junkyard **16**

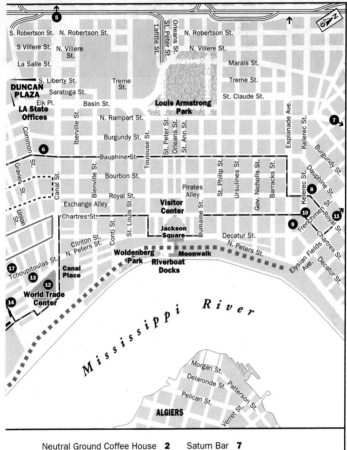

Neutral Ground Coffee House **2**

Philips Restaurant and Bar **1**

The Polo Lounge **13**

The R Bar **8**

Racketeers **1**

Rivershack Tavern **1**

Rubyfruit Jungle **10**

Rue deLa Course **18**

Saturn Bar **7**

The Sazerac Bar **6**

Snake and Jake's
  Christmas Club Lounge **1**

TJ Quills **1**

Top of the Mart Lounge **12**

Vaughan's Lounge **7**

Vic's Kangaroo Cafe **17**

Overhyped... In the southwest corner of the French Quarter lies what some locals sneer at as "Creole Disneyworld": a high-rent entertainment strip of upscale, chain theme bars, taking over one of the nation's most historic districts. No wonder preservationists are up in their *place d'arms*. In the space of a few blocks you stagger past the Fashion Cafe, House of Blues, Planet Hollywood, Hard Rock Cafe... it's enough to leave visitors wondering if they made it to New Orleans at all.

While each establishment nods to local taste, it's a garnish, not a main course. The **Hard Rock Cafe** displays music memorabilia from Professor Longhair, Fats Domino, and the Neville Brothers; **Planet Hollywood**'s museum of movie props and costumes emphasizes films set in the South and Louisiana; most significant, the **House of Blues** can boast the city's most stellar live music schedule, with recent appearances by Eric Clapton and Bob Dylan, as well as top artists with Louisiana ties, such as Fats Domino and Jerry Lee Lewis. But it's not enough. This proliferating theme-bar mall may be inside the boundaries of New Orleans, but it's definitely outside of this city's unique culture. At each attraction in Creole Disneyworld, the lines are a little longer, prices are a little higher, and the gift shops are a whole lot tackier. Attired in Hard Rock T-shirts and House of Blues jean jackets, the shuffling crowds often seem lost and irritated. And no wonder: they know what it means to miss New Orleans.

Also overhyped is the bar that serves more alcohol than any other drinking establishment in the United States: **Pat O'Brien's**. Unlike Creole Disneyland, Pat O's is unquestionably a local institution; the brick courtyard is lovely and the piano bar boisterous. But it's still not worth the tedious wait on St. Peter Street, which gets ridiculous on weekends or during peak tourist months. Plus, better Hurricanes can actually be found else-where—at the **Old Absinthe House Bar** or **Lafitte's Blacksmith Shop**. And you can get the souvenir glass at any gift shop in town.

Where to meet the opposite sex... It's not hard to do. New Orleanians are traditionally extroverted, and tourists who come here become even more so. This is, don't for-get, a town where people pull off their shirts and pants on the street in exchange for the right pair of plastic Mardi Gras beads. But for an honest-to-goodness pickup bar, it always helps to pay attention to a club's nickname. One stop at **Lucy's Retired Surfers' Bar** is all that's required to see why this aqua-painted tribute to all things Southern Californian is known around town as "Juicy's." An office crowd of preppy, single Uptowners or suburbanites between the ages of 25 and 35 flock here for silly but potent drinks, like the rum-based Shark Attack (complete with rubber shark) and the Danger Ranger (eat the worm for a free T-shirt). But the real attraction is the Wednesday night "Bad Girl's Club," during which mem-bers can receive an official photo I.D. and drink free in the early evening, and usually wind up dancing on the bar before it's all over.

Near Tulane and Loyola universities, **TJ Quills** and **Bruno's Bar** form two sides of a goalpost on Maple Street, and yes, college undergrads come here hoping to score. The two bars are, for all intents, interchangeable, with patrons reeling across the street (not always in a straight line) to frequent both. Few tables and long, three-sided counters keep everybody crowded together and friendly.

For somewhat more subtle experiences, **Lafitte's Blacksmith Shop** appeals to the better-mannered set, a diverse crowd of locals and tourists in their thirties and forties who fill the small, candlelit tables of this very romantic French Quarter bar. While Lucy's, TJ Quill's, and Bruno's pump up the volume with loud classic and alternative rock, the only sounds at Lafitte's are the tin-kling of keys on a 1948 Steinway, and the murmur of other conversations. And while any number of pickup lines may work at the other bars around town, at

Lafitte's customs are observed: try sending a drink over to other table.

Where to meet the same sex... While gay men and women reside throughout New Orleans, the French Quarter is home to an especially vibrant and visible gay community, whose members own much of the residential property and support a number of gay-owned bars, dance clubs, bookstores, laundromats, grocers, and restaurants. Even the straights attend gay events down here, including the very popular Mardi Gras gay fashion show and the annual Easter bonnet parade. Many of these civic events are sponsored by **Good Friends**, a casual neighborhood bar in the Quarter. The regular crowd befits the name—this may be the easiest place in the world to start a conversation. French doors are flung open to the street in nice weather, and a cozy gas fireplace burns in the back room in the cold months. Open 24 hours, the bar's personality changes hourly. A 6 to 10am happy hour brings in a mix of late-night carousers and early-morning red-eyes. Locals and tourists filter in throughout the day, and evening kicks off with an after-work happy hour from 4 to 6pm. The night crowd can get rowdy and pretty loose—except for the Thursday night dart tournament in the upstairs **Queen's Head Pub**, which is serious business. More dressy is **Lucky Cheng's**, an offshoot of the New York restaurant of the same name. The high-camp concept is the same in both cities, with Asian-American drag queens serving up nouvelle Asian cooking to a mix of gay and straight locals and wide-eyed tourists. The bar attracts locals with a two-for-one happy hour from 5 to 7pm; it's also recommended for a post-prandial nightcap. If you want a quicker picker-upper, the raucous **Bourbon Pub** is a video bar with a nightly lineup of pop and high-energy vids and occasional dancers on the bar top. With the **Parade** dance club directly above it and another, **Oz**, across Bourbon Street (see The Club Scene for details on both), this is the hottest action in the French Quarter.

For 20 years, **Charlene's** has been the late-night destination of choice for New Orleans' lesbians. Ring the door to be buzzed into an attractive bar with cozy booths, bamboo chairs and tables, and a vivid, rainbow-colored tile floor that dates back further than anyone can remember. A diverse crowd of women wanders in to shoot pool under strobe lights, watch sports events with beer and hot dogs, get lost in conversation, or wake up on Sunday morning with the bartender's beloved spicy Bloody Marys. On the last Saturday of each month, the pool table is pushed back for "Viva Las Vamps," a fun all-female revue. Charlene's is getting a run for its money, however, from the new kid on the block, the lively, woman-owned **Rubyfruit Jungle**, which is very popular with twentysomething women, as well as open-minded gay and straight men. This clean, chrome bar in the Faubourg Marigny has track lights, a good sound system for techno and house dances on weekends, a red pool table in the front window, fishbowls of rainbow-colored condoms, and nightly specials that include cheap oysters, country-western line dancing, and occasional live acoustic music. This is one of the city's friendliest bars to meet the same sex, opposite sex, or any combination thereof. The club's motto: "Check your prejudice at the door."

Outdoor spots for those Southern nights... The daylight hours are to be endured during a New Orleans summer; people swim through the hot, humid mornings and afternoons, muddy-headed and forever blotting trickles of perspiration from their brows and looking for a Freon buzz from the nearest air conditioner. But at dusk, the city slowly re-emerges, as people come out to sit on their balconies, courtyards, stoops, and porches, drinking in the fresh air and replenishing their lost liquids.

Not surprisingly, a patio or courtyard where you can lounge outside and sip a cold one can be a bar's most popular feature on summer nights. Uptown at the **Columns Hotel**, the front patio between the hotel's namesake pillars has comfortable metal tables covered with red tablecloths. As you look over the oak tree canopies of St. Charles Avenue, green streetcars rumble back and forth in front of you like your own model train. Also Uptown is the lively **F&M Patio Bar**, a 50-year-old neighborhood bar that packs in both locals and college students on the back patio. A strange, potted-plant greenhouse lines one wall, and there's even an outdoor pool table.

The ever-popular **Pat O'Brien's** boasts one of the city's most lush, attractive patios, with tables centered around a gurgling fountain while ivy climbs up the brick walls. But the wait can be frustrating, and once you're in, the crowd seems to breathe down your neck. Your cocktail server is thinking about table turnover and never fully allows you to relax under the stars. In summertime, however—the slack tourist season—Pat O's can be a real pleasure. Smaller but no less stately is the courtyard at the landmark **Napoleon House Bar and Cafe**, where French doors are thrown open in summer and front tables overlook the street. After one Pimm's Cup, you'll feel your heart rate slow, and the soles of your feet will start to cool.

Hippest... Look around at your compatriot barflies at **Snake and Jake's Christmas Club Lounge**. If they look at all familiar, it may be because a photographer from a supermarket tabloid reportedly haunts this Uptown joint, and frequently snaps his friends to be the next three-headed baby or Elvis sighter. This funky new bar was opened by some local musicians, and on Monday before Mardi Gras they host a "dud fest" for bands who can't find a gig. A great jukebox and dark nooks for late-night conversation are the draw, and the holiday decor includes strings of Christmas lights, a dusty plastic tree, and maniacally grinning Santas. The goatees in attendance are getting a touch of grey: the crowd is mostly in their thirties. **The R Bar**, in the Faubourg Marigny has a younger clientele, many of them hotel and restaurant workers who've come to spend their tips. The decor could be called retro-lounge lizard, with a Triumph motorcycle parked on the fridge; leopard prints covering the circa-fifties furniture; and lounge, surf, klezmer, and rockabilly on the juke box. Monday night "hair saloons" feature a shot and a haircut for ten bucks.

Finally, on weekends, those in the know join the **Saturn Bar**'s regular crowd out in the blue-collar Ninth Ward. They play all the Sinatra on the jukebox, drink longnecks of Dixie, shoot pool, and occasionally bump into celebrities like Sam Shepard or Sean Penn, who reportedly retreated here to get away from the opening ceremonies of Planet Hollywood.

Best beer selection... Beery-eyed college students and twentysomething professionals in khaki shorts and Nikes pack **The Bulldog** nightly for a pull from more than fifty spigots of draft beer or a choice from more than two hundred international varieties by the bottle. The glasses are all chilled, making for a frequent sound of breaking glass when things get rowdy late at night at this small Uptown bar, which is often packed shoulder-to-shoulder. Very loud alternative rock is on the speakers and an interactive network trivia game plays on the monitors. Looking around, you get the feeling that the smorgasbord beer selection is mostly for show, and that these guys would drink a pitcher of whatever was set before them. If the goal is to rival the United Nations in beer countries, **Cooter Brown's**, that friendly Riverbend hangout, has the edge over the Bulldog, weighing in with lagers from Korea, Lebanon, Turkey, Wales, and Nigeria, among other countries. Cooter's even offers a free T-shirt to anyone who completes a "passport" by buying a brew from 36 consecutive countries. Other bars beloved for their draft beer selection are **Carrollton Station**, a laid-back neighborhood bar located across the street from the streetcar barn Uptown, and the **Rivershack Tavern** out in Jefferson, which attracts upscale bikers on Wednesdays for its buck-and-a-half pint special.

Better after 2am... With no last call and not enough Protestants to have a work ethic, this can be a very late town. Most bars and music clubs don't really start rolling until 11pm or midnight, and many nightspots have acquired a reputation as the place to go after you've been everywhere else. But only **The Dungeon** (aka Ye Olde Original Dungeon) waits till the midnight hour to throw open its creaky doors. Imagine a haunted house, amusement park–style: a narrow passageway leads to the first bar, which is blanketed in *faux* spider webbing. A tiny staircase leads to another bar and a small dance floor upstairs. Classic and progressive rock plays at loud decibels; this French Quarter dive is a favorite haunt for visiting rock bands (Aerosmith stopped in on a recent visit). Upstairs, one section called the "cage" is the only place off the security camera's monitoring system: it's an open invitation for all kinds of depravity, which—the bouncer promised—actually occur from time to time.

The clientele includes heavy metal freaks, bikers, and thrillseekers.

A little more understated are **The R Bar** and **Snake and Jake's Christmas Club Lounge**. Both bars attract young, goateed lounge lizards. Much of The R Bar's regular, younger crowd lives in the funky Faubourg Marigny neighborhood and works in French Quarter bars and restaurants—this is a popular after-shift hangout. Uptown, Snake & Jake's offers an old-sofas decor and a crowd that's a little older; musicians frequently stop by after their gigs—and occasionally get into late-night jam sessions. Also Uptown, **Le Bon Temps Roule** and the **F&M Patio Bar** really start rocking after 2am, when the back patio photo booth starts flashing at Le Bon Temps and people start dancing on the pool table at F&M. **Audubon Tavern II** stays lively later than the other Uptown college bars, maybe because it's the only one where people dance, most of them doing the "drunken twist." This is also the rowdiest college bar, with a deserved reputation for late-night brawls, and a parking lot that frequently doubles as a giant, non-flushing urinal.

Putting on the Ritz... When it comes to dressing to the nines, New Orleans tends more to the laissez faire than the savoir-faire; it's fairly common to see someone in shorts and a T-shirt even in a stately landmark bar like the **Napoleon House Bar and Cafe** or the **Columns**. It's also not unusual to see swank party-goers bedecked in tuxes and gowns descend on a laid-back neighborhood joint like the **Saturn Bar** or the **F&M Patio Bar**. But there remain a few choice destinations for the well-heeled to kick their heels. **The Sazerac Bar** is a favorite with the post-play and -concert set from the nearby Saenger and Orpheum theaters, who come to sip the signature Sazeracs or Ramos Gin Fizzes. The elegant, art deco room is embellished by sparkling etched glass and walled in by two murals by Paul Ninas.

The barkeep at **The Polo Lounge** reports that, following the opening of the **Fashion Cafe**, all the supermodels retreated to the Polo to smoke and drink designer water. This luxurious downtown lounge offers a gleaming grand piano, a jazz combo on weekends, and clusters of couches and plush easy chairs to sink into. Its location on the second floor of the five-diamond Windsor Court hotel means that the five-diamond **Grill Room** can supply the lounge with what has to be the city's finest bar food, including Petrosian Beluga Caviar for $120. Drink specials include a special martini made with a splash of Perrier Jouet champagne, and the humidor is well-stocked. The clientele is a mix of international hotel guests and regular patrons, all adhering to one of the few bar dress codes in town (no jeans, tennis shoes, or shorts in the evening). Polo memorabilia is also in full display at **The Bombay Club**, an Anglophile's dream in the French Quarter. As a portrait of Winston Churchill scowls from the wall, martinis are served "the British way" (chilled glasses with sprayed Vermouth) in this handsome faux-British gentlemen's club, replete with curtained tables and stuffed leather chairs.

Where to take a client... To wine and dine, and then wine again, there is nothing in town like **The Polo Lounge**, downtown in the swanky Windsor Court hotel. Resistance to any offer quickly fades as one glides across puffy carpet and sinks into a marshmallow of an easy chair. While a spider-fingered jazzman tickles the baby grand, and internationals speak in tongues all around you, sip the Polo Lounge martini, made with Perrier Jouet champagne. After the handshake, call for the freestanding wooden humidor stuffed with celebratory cigars.

For private negotiations, **The Bombay Club**, that French Quarter bastion of British clubbiness, offers tables with pull curtains, along with classic martinis and a good wine list. Only a bit more laid-back is the **Bayou Bar** in the Garden District's Pontchartrain Hotel, a quiet wood and brick room decorated with stately paintings by Reineke. Drink specials include single malt scotch, Sazeracs, and tangy margaritas. Of course, if you want to promise somebody the key to the city, the **Top of the Mart Lounge**—towering 33 stories above the ground with a fabulous view of New Orleans—is the place to go. But take heed: with red plush chairs, 136 tiny tables with flickering candles, red curtains with gold cords, red and black carpet, and engorged chandelier, this downtown lounge is over the top in more ways than one, and may not appeal to everyone's taste.

NEW ORLEANS ⟋ THE BAR SCENE

Where young professionals hang... The economy of New Orleans hasn't really created the young professional set you get in other Southern cities, such as Dallas or Atlanta, and since slumming is a way of life here, many of the day's suits get put away at night. But clubs downtown (along with the nearby Warehouse District) do a thriving early-evening business with after-work locals who don't want to fight the traffic to the suburbs. Of them, **Lucy's Retired Surfers' Bar** rocks the hardest and loudest, and has the youngest and trendiest clientele. Gimmicky drink specials include the "Shark Attack," which reenacts Jaws right in your glass—your server will even sing the *bm-mm, bm-mm* theme song. Down the street, things are a little more low-key at **Vic's Kangaroo Cafe**, where Australian beers, wines by the glass, and food are served to the after-work crowd. Neither sharks nor much glamor here; Vic's is a friendly place to loosen your tie or let your hair down.

Also downtown, **Ernst Cafe** attracts customers ranging from lawyers to office workers from the nearby shipping, hotel, and construction industries. This quiet conversation bar has the oldest crowd of the downtown professional destinations ("Lucy's is for kids," opined one patron). Pressed-tin walls, mosaic tile floors, and an old cherry wood bar top give Ernst a classic New Orleans ambiance. Frilly drinks, such as Pink Squirrels and White Russians, are popular, and Saturday is ladies' night. By the way, don't be alarmed when you enter: the strange designs in the century-old tile are not inverted swastikas, as several signs hasten to point out, but ancient symbols that predate the sign of the Third Reich.

Away from the downtown area, the **Columns Hotel** on St. Charles Avenue attracts professionals (especially from medicine and law) who're looking for something a little funkier than the downtown bars. Tables line the front patio, and the inside bar has plenty of nooks and crannies for conversation. The interior ambiance is stately, with a hint of decay: appointments include a 150-year-old oak canopy; stained glass windows; 12-foot-tall, 300-pound doors; and musty pillows and cracked chair cushions that provide a whiff of the decadent South. And in the French Quarter, Thursday night is media night at the rollicking Irish bar **Molly's at the Market**. Local media personalities and politicians make guest appearances behind the bar, and that guy you're spilling your guts to might be the next governor of Louisiana.

For the college set... Most of the Uptown bars bring in some of the Tulane and Loyola crowd, especially the beer—happy **Bulldog**, preppy **Le Bon Temps Roule**, casual **Cooter Brown's,** and the rowdy **Audubon Tavern II**. But those aren't really college bars. A real college bar has: 1) a strange collection of arcana on the walls; 2) more bar space than tables, because the clientele is more interested in meeting people than dealing with the ones they walked in with; 3) a location within staggering distance of campus; 4) very gross bathrooms at the end of the night.

The Boot, TJ Quills, and Bruno's all qualify. **The Boot** sits directly between Tulane campus and fraternity row, in a complex that also includes a late-night used record store and a coffee stand (what more could a kid ask for?). A lot goes on here, including movie nights and occasional live bands, and you'll find a few grad students and profs stopping by in the early evening. Down on Maple Street, **TJ Quills** and **Bruno's** are both prototypical college bars. There are few differences between the two: they throw darts in Bruno's and shoot pool at TJ's. Both are enormously popular, perfect for wearing your jeans and Greek letters, trying out your new fake ID, and hoping to score. On two separate visits to TJ's, the men's bathroom was sprayed with someone's misfortune. The tiny patio of Bruno's gives the distinct sensation of having a kegger on someone's driveway.

A couple blocks up Maple Street, the more laid-back **Philips Restaurant & Bar** is popular with a slightly older crowd of grad and law students. The first room is devoted to a big-screen sports TV; the second landing has a pool table; nearly hidden from view is a back room that has the alluring decor of a cut-rate bordello of old. Everything is red and black, including the bar and a fake leather make-out couch in the corner.

For sports fans... Most neighborhood bars switch on the television dial to watch playoffs, bowl games, and other major sporting events, and food and drink specials are usually offered for the occasion. But the fact that New Orleans is not a major sports town is underscored by the location of its two biggest sports bars: in hotels, where out-of-town sports fans congregate. Connected by a series of carpeted corridors to the main building of the Hilton Riverside, **Kabby's Sports Edition & Grille** is a sports bar dropped down in the middle of what seems like an upscale mall of restaurants and hotel gift shops. But in the bar, the crowd is suitably noisy, stomping feet on wooden floors and pounding on the tables during scores. An impressive display of sports memorabilia lines the walls, and the basket of popcorn never empties. Rows of televisions—52 in all—are spread throughout the bar, and they broadcast from three satellites. The Hyatt Hotel's proximity to the Superdome makes **Hyttops** the place to be after a Saints game or during events such as the Sugar Bowl. Other sports events are aired on seven big-screen TVs. Near the Tulane and Loyola campuses, **Philips Restaurant & Bar** isn't really a sports bar, but a big-screen TV occupies center stage in the main room, and a devoted crowd gathers to watch football, basketball, boxing, and such. And if your idea of football is a round, black-and-white ball you can't touch with your hands, **Fritzel's European Jazz Club** in the French Quarter screens all the major European matches for a suitably rowdy pub crowd.

For active sports, there's nothing within the city limits quite like the **Buffalo Beach Club**. An outdoor, regulation-size volleyball court with eight inches of sand sits like a mirage amid downtown buildings and parking lots; volleyball tournaments start up in the spring, usually on Tuesdays and Thursdays. When the court's open, it's first come, first serve. Buffalo's also has pool tables and a big-screen TV that is tuned to sports, but the concept hasn't completely caught on, and the place is apt to be near-empty on many nights.

Most bars have one or two pool tables—**Philips** and **Cooter Brown's** Uptown, and **Check Point Charlie's** and **Rubyfruit Jungle** in the Faubourg Marigny are some of the most appealing. But the most serious sharks head out to suburban Jefferson to infest the waters at **Racketeer's**, which provides 25 regulation tables in an austere, shut-up-and-play environment that's popular on weekends with slacking college students. Tables rent for hourly rates.

Historical interest... The hand-scrawled letters are barely visible on the back wall of **Lafitte's Blacksmith Shop** on Bourbon Street. But if you look close, you can discern a French phrase that reads, in translation: "Love passes with time. Time passes with love." The romance-minded graffiti artist may have lived during the bar's early days in the late eighteenth century, but the manager says he doesn't intend to take any steps to preserve the lettering: "Let it fade," he mutters, as he turns to prepare another drink. This quiet cocktail bar dates to 1772, and after the Ursuline Convent, it's the oldest structure in the French Quarter. It shows—but the crumbling woodframe, brick, and plaster only enhance the mystique of the bar. In 1809, the smithy was bought by the infamous Jean Lafitte, who used this as a front to sell his pirated booty. Also in a carefully maintained state of disrepair, the **Napoleon House**, a certified National Historic Landmark, dates to 1821, when Napoleon was languishing on St. Helena island while a bunch of scheming French expatriates (including Jean Lafitte and New Orleans Mayor Nicholas Girod) plotted to spirit the defeated emperor to safe haven. Girod built an addition to his house, and ships were readied, but Napoleon died before he could escape to the home that now bears his name (along with a bust positioned strategically over the cash register). Dating back to 1806, the **Old Absinthe House Bar** is one of the oldest continually operated drinking establishments in the country. You can literally read the history of the bar on its walls: The rows of dollar bills recall World War II, when New Orleans was a major shipping-out point, and enlisted men tacked up dollars for good luck before they hit the seas. Higher on the wall are nicotine-coated dueling cards, which men of honor once presented each other after they had been insulted. (Fencing matches were held either behind St. Louis Cathedral in St. Anthony's Garden, or in City Park, beneath the "Dueling Oaks.")

If you scratch any New Orleans tavern hard enough, you'll probably find some strange and possibly nefarious history. Downtown, the **Ernst Cafe** was once a bordello, and the "cribs" (prostitutes' rooms) are still visible in the second-story interior brickwork. As its name suggests, **Racketeers**, out in Jefferson, was once an old gambling casino called the Southport Club. The stories go that Bugsy Siegel once ran the joint, and that Governor Huey Long himself had a piece of the action. In the office, a massive cement vault and a trapdoor (for escape during raids) testify to the rough old days. But not all of New Orleans' history is pirates, prostitutes, and gangsters: The now-campy **Rivershack Tavern** out in Jefferson and Uptown's **Le Bon Temps Roule** were turn-of-the-century neighborhood apothecaries, and in the sidewalk outside Faubourg Marigny's **The R Bar** is the inscription "Hank was here 1955," which was carved by the poet Charles Bukowski. At least that's what everyone says, and who wants to let the facts get in the way of a good legend?

Worth the drive... You'll need either a car or a hefty investment in cab fare, but for intrepid explorers wishing to venture out into the city, here are some worthy nighttime destinations. First stop: the Ninth Ward, a blue-collar neighborhood with its own way of living, talking, and partying. The unofficial checkpoint into the Ninth Ward is the **Saturn Bar**. The interior of this mausoleum-like building is plastered in layers of posters, pictures, and a special genre of art that can only be called thriftstore–Gothic. There are some wonderful neon relics here, including the candy turtle (ask to have it turned on). The clientele varies wildly, but there are usually about three older men at the bar, drinking bottled beer and watching the exercise channel. Not far from the Saturn is a more modest neighborhood bar, **Vaughan's Lounge**, a two-room corner joint known for its street party on Independence Day. It's been quietly gaining city-wide popularity; crowds gather to hear jazz trumpeter Kermit Ruffins on Thursdays, and to plow through plates of crawfish on Fridays. Other days, the clientele is a combo of neighborhood regulars, wayfaring students, bikers, and military personnel from a nearby base.

A 15-minute drive along River Road into the suburb of Jefferson leads to the campy and kitschy **Rivershack Tavern**. The Rivershack's penchant for gimmicks includes a tacky ashtray collection that increases daily—customers bring new objets d'art, which are evaluated with a jeweler's precision and exchanged for drinks. Be sure to check out the "Bar Legs" barstools, which lend their occupants the legs of golfers, baseball players, and cowboys. The very good late-night kitchen, extensive beer menu, and excellent martinis and margaritas attract a diverse crowd: professionals in their thirties and forties, college students, and music fans (live bands play weekend nights). Wednesday nights, the $1.50 pint special makes this the city's premiere upscale biker bar.

Rivaling the Saturn and Rivershack for decorative strangeness is the well-titled **My Father's Junkyard**. This spacious bar is filled with decorations brought in from a real junkyard, which did in fact belong to the owner's dad. Included in the catalogue: a '58 Dodge, rows of hubcaps, Tonka trucks, dollhouses, artificial Christmas trees, and stuffed bunnies. The clientele is mostly in their forties and fifties, although young Junkyard fans make their way here on weekends. The bar is located across the river from New Orleans, on the West Bank. It's accessible by bridge or the Jackson ferry, which is an adventure in itself. (Call the bar for ferry directions.)

Hold the pretzels: boiled crawfish and raw oysters... That large, purple mesh sack moving by the doorway isn't some creature from a horror flick. It's filled with live crawfish, and it's a sure sign you're at a good New Orleans party. A crawfish boil is one of those roll-up-your-sleeves affairs: the craws are boiled live with bags of garlic and spices, and served very informally on a newspaper-covered table, along with boiled potatoes, corn, garlic flowers, and—at fancy events—artichokes. Learning to pinch the tail (to remove the shell) and suck the head (the best part, locals say) is a rite of passage, and either your bartender or someone next to you at the table will be perversely proud to offer instructions. During crawfish season—late January to June—the mudbugs are served Friday afternoons at many locations throughout town. A real casual, down-home boil can be found at the neighborhoody **Vaughan's Lounge** out in the Ninth Ward. Meanwhile, the college crowd peels out at **TJ Quills**, that permanent floating frat party on Maple Street. And the **Buffalo Beach Club** boils them for a varied group of neighborhood regulars and professionals from nearby downtown.

Like crawfish, raw oysters require a certain amount of bravery the first time you try them: even if you like the taste, there's that slippery texture to contend with. It helps to douse the oyster liberally in either homemade cocktail sauce or a concoction of catsup, horseradish, and Tabasco (the bar will provide the ingredients). Many first-timers place the oyster on a saltine cracker, also available at the bar. The oyster bar is usually conjoined to the drink bar, and at many locations, a dozen of the little bivalves are considered as natural as a round of drinks.

One of the most popular oyster bars is Uptown at **Cooter Brown's**, one of New Orleans's most popular taverns, offering pool, darts, a humidor of cigars, and beers of all nations to a friendly crowd of students and young professionals. At Cooter's oyster bar, the quality is high and the price relatively low. The price is lower still at **Rubyfruit Jungle**, a friendly lesbian bar in the Faubourg Marigny that serves oysters for a quarter on Monday nights. Then there's **Le Bon Temps Roule**, a funky Uptown bar that undersells them all: Friday is "Shuck and Jive Night," which hooks a large crowd by using two sure baits: free oysters and live music.

Where to drink a Hurricane... The first trip to **Pat O'Brien's** is a treasured memory for many New Orleanians. In days past, no high school graduation was complete without a trip to Pat O's for a gigantic "Magnum": a Hurricane served with several long straws, with enough libation for a table of drinkers. As the story goes, the practice was discontinued after a particularly rowdy weekend when warring fans of LSU and Tulane football teams began tossing the glasses across the patio at one another. Hurricane consumption is now limited to 29 ounces at a time, but the crowds still press into Pat O's for what is the most famous, if not necessarily the best, Hurricane in town.

Pat O'Brien's has even packaged its Hurricane mix, and most other bars in town use it for their Hurricanes. But not all of them do, and the exceptions are definitely worth going out of your way to try. Hurricanes from scratch can be found at the **Old Absinthe House Bar** or **Lafitte's Blacksmith Shop** (both on Bourbon Street), which forego the instant mix for a blend of fresh juices and light and dark rums, or at the swanky **Polo Lounge** downtown, which uses three kinds of rums. The difference is appreciable.

Where to drink a Sazerac... Most classic New Orleans bars serve Sazeracs, and the **Old Absinthe House Bar** offers one of the best. For extra ambience, this vintage French Quarter bar still has on display an authentic absinthe drip, complete with a well-worn limestone base. But as one might expect, the eponymous **Sazerac Bar** downtown in the Fairmont Hotel is generally regarded as the place to go for a textbook Sazerac. The copper-colored cocktail is the same hue as this classy, art-deco-style hotel bar.

Where to drink a Ramos Gin Fizz... This sweet, delicate, frothy mixture with a hint of citrus was an invention of the old Roosevelt Hotel. Today, the Fairmont is located on the Roosevelt's site, and its **Sazerac Bar** is still the home of the Ramos. The drink also plays a part in Louisiana's history. Both the Roosevelt and the Ramos were favorites of Louisiana's notorious governor, Huey Long. In fact, T. Harry Williams, in his definitive biography of the Guv (titled *Huey Long*) tells the story of a day in 1935 when Long, then a U.S. Senator, introduced the Ramos Gin Fizz to New York. As Williams tells the tale, Long staged a "bizarre publicity stunt" at the New Yorker hotel during which he declared that the Big Apple had no acceptable gin fizzes. Then the Senator introduced Sam Guarino, who was the Roosevelt's head bartender, to the reporters. Guarino prepared five Ramos Gin Fizzes; Long downed each of them, proclaiming, "This is, gentlemen, my gift to New York." The New York press ridiculed the buffoonish event, but Williams surmises that Long had the last laugh, and that he was "clowning to divert attention from a serious effort he had to make to prevent the federal Treasury from sabotaging the sale of... Louisiana bonds." Sadly, Ramos Gin Fizzes are becoming a rare commodity in New Orleans, and the **Napoleon House** has discontinued the drink. The Fairmont is still your best bet. The bartender at the **Carousel** also observes the proper preparation (stirred, not shaken). Such care is necessary, of course, to convey the right amount of nostalgia for the old days when politics and potables were both stirred up by Louisiana's most infamous leader.

NEW ORLEANS ⟨ THE BAR SCENE

Best summer coolants... While Napoleon himself might not be amused, the establishment that bears his name is best known for a British-born drink, the Pimm's Cup—so well known, in fact, that the **Napoleon House** even sells a do-it-at-home Pimm's gift set. **Pat O'Brien's** floats a half-dozen fresh mint leaves in the bourbon-sugar water pool of its mint juleps, and the Sazerac Bar also keeps fresh mint on hand. While **Top of the Mart**, the revolving bar atop the International Trade Mart, doesn't use fresh mint, fans of syrup-sweet drinks will appreciate its juleps anyway.

Lead your own movie tour... If your surroundings look strangely familiar, it may be because you've seen them on celluloid. Over the years, many movies and TV shows have been filmed in New Orleans, and some local bars play feature roles.

Of course, a local movie tour might as well start at **Planet Hollywood**, which is pretty much like all the other members of the Planet Hollywood chain, except that it does have a nice collection of New Orleans-related movie costumes and props, such as Marlene Dietrich's dress from *The Flame of New Orleans*, Bette Davis' petticoat from *Jezebel*, and a fake alligator from *Interview with the Vampire*.

From there, check out three bars that had bit roles in recent films. The Faubourg Marigny's **Check Point Charlie's** appeared in *The Pelican Brief*—Julia Roberts did her laundry in the bar's back room. In the same film, **Kaldi's Coffeehouse** in the French Quarter played a bank (which, incidentally, it once was in real life). And in Oliver Stone's *JFK*, Kevin Costner was seen retreating to the historic **Napoleon House** to watch the president's assassination on TV.

Certainly the most recognizable movie set in town is the **Columns Hotel**, a symbol of the decadent South featured prominently in *Pretty Baby*, Louis Malle's controversial film about New Orleans' red-light district of Storyville. Inside, the Columns' bar has a photo display of *Pretty Baby*'s star, Brooke Shields. The real Storyville, of course, is long gone.

Suds & suds: where to get a drink during the spin cycle... "No, I can't go out because I have to do my laundry" is no longer an acceptable excuse to stay home. In addition to being the city's best no-cover rock 'n' roll and blues venue, a 24-hour bar and grill, and a paperback book exchange, **Check Point Charlie's** is the world's darkest and smokiest laundromat, with eight machines in a small room behind the stage. On the other end of the Quarter, the multi-purpose **Hula Mae's Tropic Wash & Beach Cafe** is more than just a fun place to wash your socks—it's actually quite a happening nightspot, albeit more brightly lit than most, and with a fresh detergent scent in the air. In addition to washing machines, dry-cleaning, and P.O. boxes, Hula Mae's offers the city's first barroom computer terminal. The crowd is evenly mixed between locals and tourists, and gay and straight, all of whom make it here each Monday to drink bottled beer and wine coolers and watch "Melrose Place."

Microbreweries, beer gardens, and wine bars...

The gleaming wood and brass appointments of the **Crescent City Brewhouse** are clean and crisp, as is the very fine beer that pours from those shiny tanks behind the bar. In addition to four beers brewed on premises, Crescent City has a decent oyster bar and a menu that's a little heavier on salads and vegetables than most local spots. There's not much of a scene here: mostly tourists wandering by from the Jax Brewery shopping mall. But it's worth dropping by in nice weather just to sit out on the second-floor balcony and enjoy the Mississippi River view (especially if your feet are sore from trudging around the Quarter). In the more residential Mid-City neighborhood, the city's second brewpub, the small **Acadian Beer Garden**, is a better place to yak it up with the locals.

Some trends just seem to pass New Orleans by. Recently opened, **Vino! Vino!** is the city's only! only! wine bar. It's pretty much what you'd expect: a few tables and a handsome bar, and an extensive list of wines by the glass. There are weekly wine tastings, and lunch and dinner menus offer opportunities like "arugula salad with fennel, cured olives, and feta" that are notable mostly because they are so rarely found in New Orleans. The crowd is a mix of tourists and imbibing Quarterites.

Coffee bars... Whether or not you like classic New Orleans coffee depends on how you feel about two things: chicory and steamed milk. Ground chicory root is what gives this city's traditional café au lait its distinctive flavor. That's the only type of coffee available at the always-busy **Cafe du Monde Coffee Stand**, a large indoor/outdoor landmark located in the heart of the French Quarter, across Decatur Street from Jackson Square. Open 24 hours, this is one place every visitor discovers, but what the hell: it's a good place to rest your feet or write postcards, while munching on square doughnuts smothered in powdered sugar. (But don't wear black: that piled-up powdered sugar flies everywhere.)

Some locals marvel at how strong New Orleanians like their coffee, but those are people who haven't yet registered the fact that the rest of the country is drinking their coffee stronger. Coffee culture hasn't really caught on here; there's no Starbucks backlash, simply because there's no Starbucks hereabouts. Few local places serve really great brew, and they all seem to be getting their pastries from the same lousy bakery. The best cup of joe in town is Uptown at **The Daily Planet Espresso Bar**, but there's not much of a scene here, since there are only a few tables on the sidewalk and none inside. There's more activity at **Kaldi's Coffeehouse**: at any given time, the clientele in this spacious hall may include Quarter punks with spiked hair and pierced eyebrows, tarot card readers, lost tourists, and local professionals scanning today's Wall Street Journal. The coffee ice cream drinks here are especially good; the pastries are adequate.

Despite only average coffee (and those same crummy pastries), **Rue de la Course II** is the king of the Uptown coffeehouses, with a groovy hanging-out atmosphere set by jazz music and picture windows overlooking Magazine Street. Laptop-toting grad students compete for tables with game players (Scrabble, backgammon, and chess are available at the counter), and on Sundays "the Rue Two" is packed with readers of the *New York Times*, which is on sale here. The spirit of Woodstock is kept alive at the cozy, cooperatively run **Neutral Ground** in Uptown, which brings back the sixties spirit with live folk music and lots of very gentle people.

Best places to take the kids... You have to be 18 to be in a bar in Louisiana, but if it's a restaurant—or, say, a bowling alley—there's no problem. First stop: **Planet Hollywood**. Imagine the sensation of walking inside a giant television—bright and noisy and stacked with old movie props and continuous previews playing on big-screen monitors. With a bar built like an upside-down swimming pool, and nonalcoholic drinks with names like "Home Alone" and "E.T.," what more could a kid want? Well, promotional giveaways of movie merchandise and tickets, for starters. Of course, none of this has anything to do with New Orleans, but the kids could care less. They'll also be up for the **Mid-City Lanes**, a very popular bar/music club/bowling alley that provides a nice family atmosphere in the early evenings.

The Index

Acadian Beer Garden. This homey beer garden is connected to the Arcadian Brewing Company, and serves delicious, made-on-the-premises beer. Much of its customer base is nearby Mid-City residents.... *Tel 504/488–8274. 201 N. Carrollton Ave., Mid-City.*

Audubon Tavern II. At this great big two-story, wood-paneled box, a deejay spins "Louie, Louie" for Tulane and Loyola students.... *Tel 504/895–9702. 6100 Magazine St., Uptown.*

Bayou Bar. This quiet Pontchartrain Hotel lounge is a favorite of novelist Anne Rice, who features the Pontchartrain in *The Witching Hour.* Recommended bar food includes a sherry-laced Creole turtle soup.... *Tel 504/524–0581. Pontchartrain Hotel, 2031 St. Charles Ave., Garden District.*

The Bombay Club. This stately French Quarter bar offers the ambience of a British gentlemen's club, and is a favorite of stockbrokers, lawyers, and Anglophiles.... *Tel 504/586–0972. 830 Conti St., French Quarter.*

The Boot. This is the most adventurous of the undergraduate college bars, offering weekly movies and occasional live music, as well as a late-night kitchen.... *Tel 504/866–9008. 1039 Broadway, Uptown.*

Bourbon Pub. This loud, rocking video bar is located on the hottest block in town for gay men.... *Tel 504/529–2107. 801 Bourbon St., French Quarter.*

Bruno's Bar. Located within walking distance of both Tulane and Loyola campuses, this watering hole is especially popular with undergrads.... *Tel 504/861–7615. 7601 Maple St., Uptown.*

Buffalo Beach Club. Tucked away in Downtown's office buildings and parking lots is this sports bar with a sandy lot and volleyball net. It's usually not crowded, except during league play.... *Tel 504/595–8986. 867 Magazine St., Downtown.*

The Bulldog. The Tulane and Loyola undergrads who frequent this Uptown beer buffet prefer their alternative rock and Top-40 tunes at a gotta-shout-over-the-music level. Always packed, always loud.... *Tel 504/891–1516. 3236 Magazine St., Uptown.*

Cafe du Monde Coffee Stand. The famous beignets are steaming-hot and blanketed in powdered sugar, and served with chicory-laced café au lait or creamy hot chocolate. And that's it for the menu, folks.... *Tel 504/525–4544. 800 Decatur St., French Quarter. Open 24 hours.*

Carousel Bar. A New Orleans landmark since 1947, the centerpiece of this attractive hotel bar is an honest-to-God merry-go-round, complete with carved animal chairs. The carousel revolves four times each hour—so slowly that most people don't notice it until they return from the bathroom to find their drink on the other side of the bar.... *Tel 504/523–3341. 214 Royal St., French Quarter.*

Carrollton Station. This neighborhood bar located across the street from the streetcar barn has the friendly ambience of a fishing cabin. The "Dark & Stormy" (Gosling's rum and ginger beer) is a favorite. Live music (with a $5 cover) on weekends.... *Tel 504/865–9190. 8140 Willow St., Uptown.*

Charlene's. Ring the bell to be buzzed into New Orleans' most established women's bar, a cozy hangout with pool tables, strobe lights, and booths. Sundays are for Bloody Marys, and the last Saturday of each month features "Viva Las Vamps," an all-female revue.... *Tel 504/945–9328. 940 Elysian Fields Ave., Faubourg Marigny.*

Check Point Charlie's. A laundromat, lending library, bar, rock venue, pool room, and burger joint all tied up in one loud, lively, dark, and slightly dingy package. The Esplanade Avenue location means this bar does serve as a Check Point of sorts for tourists venturing into the funky Faubourg Marigny neighborhood.... *Tel 504/947–0979. 501 Esplanade Ave., Faubourg Marigny.*

Columns Hotel. The lounge here is named "The Victorian Bar." But everyone just calls it the "Columns," in honor of the sturdy pillars in front of this classic hotel. Guitarist Tony Green plays live "gypsy jazz" Tuesdays and Thursdays.... *Tel 504/899–9308. 3811 St. Charles Ave. Garden District.*

Cooter Brown's. College students and young professionals line the rows of tables in this low-key, friendly bar. The main attractions: beer from around the globe; raw oysters for cheap (less than five bucks a dozen); and cigars available for purchase at the bar.... *Tel 504/866–9104. 509 S. Carrollton Ave., Uptown.*

Crescent City Brewhouse. Silver steam rises from gleaming brass brewtanks in this handsome restaurant/bar that attracts mainly a walk-in tourist crowd.... *Tel 504/522–0571. 527 Decatur St., French Quarter.*

The Daily Planet Espresso Bar. Open until midnight on weekends, this coffee stand has outside tables that sit right in the traffic flow from Broadway's fraternity row into the Boot bar next door.... *Tel 504/866–0651. 1039 Broadway, Uptown.*

The Dungeon. It looks scary and sometimes it is. Located on a side street a few steps off Bourbon Street, this late-night metal and biker bar doesn't open until midnight.... *Tel 504/523–5530. 738 Toulouse St., French Quarter.*

Ernst Cafe. This long-standing downtown watering hole attracts an older—but not always quieter—crowd. A popular happy hour includes chances to win drink specials on the roulette wheel.... *Tel 504/525–8544. 600 S. Peters St., Downtown.*

F&M Patio Bar. Frump and Mannie's has been a New Orleans classic for a half-century, and everyone has a story about a night misspent here. There's a pool table and bar in the front room, a photo booth and vinyl couches on the side, a late-night kitchen, and a lovely outdoor patio in back.... *Tel 504/895–6784. 4841 Tchoupitoulas Ave. Uptown.*

Fashion Cafe. Owned by a bevy of supermodels, this tourist-oriented chain restaurant is the latest and most superfluous theme bar to hit the French Quarter.... *Tel 504/522–3181. 619 Decatur St., French Quarter.*

Fritzel's European Jazz Club. The setting is classic European pub, with long, wooden tables and straight-back benches. An oasis for Europeans, jazz lovers, and the Bourbon Street foot-weary.... *Tel 504/561–0432. 733 Bourbon St., French Quarter.*

Good Friends. This friendly neighborhood gay bar features a handsome mahogany arch bar, French doors, and a gas fireplace in the back room.... *Tel 504/523–9938. 740 Dauphine St., French Quarter.*

Hard Rock Cafe. New Orleans music memorabilia line the walls in this Hard Rock that's pretty much identical to those in every other major tourist destination.... *Tel 504/529–5617. 219 N. Peters St., French Quarter.*

House of Blues. The funkiest blues joint that money can buy; opened in New Orleans in January 1994. In addition to live music (and a dance club), this multimillion-dollar complex has a late-night menu, a gift shop, and a bar that serves tacky drinks, such as the "Bluesmobile" and "Blind Melon Jefferson.".... *Tel 504/529–2583. 225 Decatur St., French Quarter.*

Hula Mae's Tropic Wash & Beach Cafe. The "Hula Van" offers free shuttle service to this laundromat/cafe that serves beer and wine coolers in a tropical setting replete with neon and palm trees.... *Tel 504/522–1336. 840 N. Rampart St., French Quarter.*

Hyttops. Sports memorabilia, a collection of big-screen TVs, and proximity to the Superdome make this one of the city's few real sports bars.... *Tel 504/561–1234. Hyatt Hotel, 500 Poydras Plaza, Downtown.*

Kabby's Sports Edition & Grille. The Hilton location means this is a tourist bar, but it's still one of the best (read: most raucous) places in town to watch televised sports.... *Tel 504/584–3880. Hilton Riverside, Poydras at Mississippi River, Downtown.*

Kaldi's Coffeehouse. This handsome coffee shop, popular with everyone from gutter punks to professionals, stays open until midnight on weeknights and later on weekends, when live folk and jazz music plays.... *Tel 504/586–8989. 941 Decatur St., French Quarter.*

Lafitte's Blacksmith Shop. This crumbling, wood-frame brick-and-plaster building on upper Bourbon Street is made even more romantic by the complete absence of overhead lighting. Candles and murmured conversations provide the ambience here.... *Tel 504/523–0066. 941 Bourbon St., French Quarter.*

Le Bon Temps Roule. This funky local favorite attracts everyone from college students to neighborhood senior citizens.... *Tel 504/895–8117. 4801 Magazine St., Uptown.*

Lucky Cheng's. Asian-American transvestite waitresses; gourmet nouvelle Asian cooking, and an emphasis on campy fun that appeals to both a gay and straight crowd.... *Tel 504/529–2045. 720 St. Louis St., French Quarter.*

Lucy's Retired Surfers' Bar. This gimmick-filled bar is to liquor what Chuck E Cheese is to pizza. The owner is, yes, a retired surfer, and those really are his old boards competing with the neon in the aqua decor. The kitchen serves good California-style Mexican food.... *Tel 504/523–8995. 701 Tchoupitoulas St., Warehouse District.*

Mid–City Lanes. A bar, late-night diner, and music club in a residential neighborhood. Fun for the family on early evenings.... *Tel 504/482–3133. 4133 S. Carrollton Ave., Mid-City. About $5 cover for live music.*

Molly's at the Market. Nothing fancy here: the paint-and-graffiti splattered bathrooms look like a war zone, and the patio is also a bit grimy. But it all fits just fine into the gritty character of this popular Irish bar, a must-see on St. Pat's Day and Halloween.... *Tel 504/525–5169. 1107 Decatur St., French Quarter.*

My Father's Junkyard. Make sure your directions are straight, because this bizarre bar on the West Bank is hard to find. The name says it all: the owner's father owned a junkyard, and the bar is decorated with relics.... *Tel 504/340–1117. 350 Douglas Rd., Marrero.*

Napoleon House Bar and Cafe. Classical music, excellent food, a signature Pimm's Cup, and a slower, Old World pace that Napoleon never got to enjoy.... *Tel 504/524–9752. 500 Chartres St., French Quarter.*

Neutral Ground Coffee House. A cozy environment for conversation, chess playing, and live acoustic music. The menu: coffee, tea and pastries.... *Tel 504/891–3381. 5110 Danneel St., Uptown.*

Old Absinthe House Bar. One of the better destinations on lower Bourbon Street, this historic landmark serves authentic versions of Sazeracs, Hurricanes, and other classic cocktails. Two blocks away at 240 Bourbon Street is the similar Old Absinthe Bar, which doesn't host live music.... *Tel 504/525–8108. 400 Bourbon St., French Quarter.*

Pat O'Brien's. Expect long lines, especially during peak hours. Still, the courtyard is lovely, the piano bar is plenty rowdy, and the mandatory souvenir 29-ounce Hurricane glass is still here.... *Tel 504/525–4823. 718 St. Peter St., French Quarter.*

Philips Restaurant & Bar. The most mellow of the college bars along Maple Street near Tulane and Loyola draws more of a grad student crowd.... *Tel 504/865–1155. 733 Cherokee St., Uptown.*

Planet Hollywood. This garish theme restaurant celebrates the West Coast instead of the Gulf Coast, but is popular with kids and movie buffs.... *Tel 504/522–7826. 620 Decatur St., French Quarter.*

The Polo Lounge. This plush lounge filled with polo memorabilia, art, and plenty of blue suits is located in what is arguably the city's finest hotel.... *Tel 504/523–6000. Windsor Court Hotel, 30 Gravier St., Downtown.*

The R Bar. Riding the lounge lizard craze, the R Bar joins the Mermaid Lounge (see The Club Scene) and Snake & Jake's as a new hot spot for young hipsters. The inn next door is popular with European travelers.... *Tel 504/948–7499. 1431 Royal St., Faubourg Marigny.*

Racketeers. The city's most serious pool hall has a stark environment and offers drink specials, like "El Mafioso Coffee," that honor its seedy past as an illegal casino.... *Tel 504/ 840–7665. 200 Monticello Ave., Jefferson.*

Rivershack Tavern. In an unlikely location facing the Mississippi River levee and nestled among various industrial yards, this kitschy hangout is one of the city's most interesting and friendly neighborhood bars.... *Tel 504/834–4938. 3449 River Rd., Jefferson.*

Rubyfruit Jungle. The many attractions at this woman-owned gay bar include fishbowls of brightly colored condoms, a red felt pool table, oysters for a quarter on Mondays, country music line dancing, drag shows, techno and house music dancing.... *Tel 504/947–4000. 640 Frenchmen St., Faubourg Marigny.*

Rue de la Course II. Open until midnight on weekends, this large, bustling coffeehouse is especially popular with older students and board game players. "Rue One" is smaller and located a few blocks down Magazine.... *Tel 504/899–0242. 3128 Magazine St., Uptown.*

Saturn Bar. This funky two-story landmark in the Ninth Ward has displayed the same strange art and snapshots on the walls for about 40 years.... *Tel 504/949–7532. 3067 St. Claude Ave., Ninth Ward.*

The Sazerac Bar. This tiny, art-deco hotel bar is home court to one of New Orleans' most favorite drinks, the Sazerac. This bar caters to local businesspeople during the day, and the symphony and Saenger crowds at night.... *Tel 504/529–4733. The Fairmont Hotel, 123 Baronne St., Downtown.*

Snake and Jake's Christmas Club Lounge. This Uptown dive opened in 1995 and is currently the hottest watering hole for local artists and musicians. This is also one of the wildest sites (and sights) at Mardi Gras.... *Tel 504/861–2802. 7612 Oak St., Uptown.*

TJ Quills. Right across the street from the very similar Bruno's, this run-of-the-mill college bar, dressed up like an ersatz hunting lodge, packs in the Greeks.... *Tel 504/866–5205. 7600 Maple St., Uptown.*

Top of the Mart Lounge. The largest revolving bar or restaurant in the country will turn you in one complete circle every 90 minutes as you gaze down on the Crescent City's crescent and all those little people 33 floors below.... *Tel 504/522–9795. International Trade Mart, Downtown.*

Vaughan's Lounge. This amiable neighborhood bar is located off the beaten track, near a military base in the city's blue-collar Ninth Ward. Friday night crawfish boils and Thursday night jazz with trumpeter Kermit Ruffins are popular draws.... *Tel 504/947–5562. 800 Lesseps St., Ninth Ward.*

Vic's Kangaroo Cafe. Don't try to tell the Australia-born owner that the Down Under fad went out with Crocodile Dundee. Late nights are also popular, with live blues bands on week-ends.... *Tel 504/524–4329. 636 Tchoupitoulas St., Warehouse District.*

Vino! Vino! The Crescent City's only wine bar offers a list of over 40 wines by the glass—red, white, sweet, or bubbly. The bright, pristine decor is based around a long, yellow-painted bar.... *Tel 504/529–4553. 1119 Decatur St., French Quarter.*

mardi gras

3

& jazz fest

Consider it a party with three million of your closest friends. A count made in 1995 found the number of people who stood on a street to watch a Mardi Gras parade was something like 3,570,100. Or here's another tally, following the conventional wisdom that the success of each Mardi Gras is measured in the amount of trash swept up the next day: toward the end of the eighties, over 2,000 tons were collected each year.

And then there's Jazz Fest, seven days in April or May when music overruns this music-loving city. Orleanians used to say that Mardi Gras is the party we throw for the world, and Jazz Fest is the party we throw just for ourselves: Well, not anymore. Each year, the Fest breaks a new record in daily attendance.

If you're trying to choose between Mardi Gras or Jazz Fest, compare and contrast the two big events. For both, hotel rooms fill up months in advance. Clubs charge about twice the price for admission, and many restaurants start serving "special" (read: higher prices) menus. During Mardi Gras, everyone starts wearing plastic necklaces day and night, and people start pulling off their clothes in public. Also, the music gets better. During Jazz Fest, the music just gets better. You decide.

The What, When, and Where of Mardi Gras

Literally meaning "Fat Tuesday," Mardi Gras is, supposedly, the last chance for Catholics to bid farewell to fleshly pleasure before undertaking the Lenten season of abstinence. But just as everyone is Irish on St. Pat's Day, anyone in New Orleans is Catholic on Mardi Gras. Across the city, people get into the act in all sorts of ways: college students flash beads on Bourbon Street; gay men parade about in outlandish drag; African-American men (and a few women) dress as Mardi Gras Indians; and suburban families set up little roadside towns of folding chairs and ladders to watch the passing parade.

Mardi Gras is the day before Ash Wednesday, which is determined by the church calendar. But Carnival season actually begins on January 6, or Twelfth Night. That's when parades start to roll on a regular basis. Crowds pour into town on the weekend before Fat Tuesday, which is the time for public and private balls (see below) and the start of a non-stop voyeur's orgy that's concentrated on Bourbon Street. **Lundi Gras** is the night before Fat Tuesday, which civic leaders have been trying hard to promote as another major party night.

Each day during Carnival season, the daily *Times-Picayune* publishes parade route maps. The daily also publishes a special Mardi Gras magazine at the beginning of the season, and the Friday "Lagniappe" entertainment guide of the newspaper is a good source for special events and club shows. The *Gambit Weekly* also has an annual guide with parade maps and ratings. Locals wait for these editions to hit the stands two weeks before Carnival Day and quickly snap them up. Easier to find is Arthur Hardy's *Mardi Gras Guide* (tel 504/838–6111), a glossy magazine that's sold for about three bucks in grocery stores and newsstands throughout the city. It's filled with parade maps, Mardi Gras history, and feature articles about float builders, costumers, and other behind-the-scenes people. If you're planning a Mardi Gras trip, keep in mind that everything from concert tickets to car rentals should be booked two to three months in advance. Hotel reservations should be made six months early or more, for prime parade and Bourbon Street spots.

The What, When, and Where of Jazz Fest

Officially called the **New Orleans Jazz and Heritage Festival** (tel 504/522–4786; 1205 N. Rampart St., Treme), Jazz Fest takes place over seven days, spanning the last weekend of April and first weekend of May. Besides the daytime music lineup at the **Fair Grounds** (1751 Gentilly Blvd., Mid-City), the Jazz Fest has a stellar evening concert schedule, with major headliners usually performing a longer show in a large venue, such as the **Lakefront Arena** (University of New Orleans, 6801 Franklin Ave., Lakefront) or the **Convention Center** (900 Convention Center Blvd., Downtown). These shows go late: they commonly include two other performers, and the main attraction may not take the stage until after midnight. Seating is often reserved; ticket prices range from $20 to $35. Tickets are available by phone through **Ticketmaster** (tel 504/522–5555 or 800/488–5252), which also handles tickets for many other major Fest-time shows, including those at **Tipitina's** (tel 504/895–8477; 501 Napoleon Ave., Uptown). **The House of Blues** (tel 504/529–1421; 225 Decatur St., French Quarter) also sells advance tickets; hot shows such as the Neville Brothers usually sell out long before the night of the concert.

Only first-timers to the Fest purchase the official guide, which is sold inside the Fair Grounds. Everyone else knows that the best Jazz Fest guide by far is published by *OffBeat*: handed out free every day in front of the Fair Grounds, it features in-depth interviews with dozens of musicians, plus an insert schedule printed on heavy paper stock, which is perfect for tearing out and keeping in your back pocket. If you can find it, the free *Gambit Weekly* is the only publication that publishes detailed reviews and ratings of each act that's playing the Fest. Finally, online Jazz Fest info can be found through *OffBeat*'s website (http://www.neosoft.com/~offbeat). **Jazz Fest's web-site** (http://www.nojazzfest.com) also has chats with artists.

The Lowdown

Where to get your Mardi Gras costume... For bargain-hunters, the costume racks at **Thrift City** (tel 504/482–0736; 4125 S. Carrollton Ave., Mid-City) are the stuff of legends. As Mardi Gras approaches, this demure thrift store in a residential Mid-City neighborhood becomes a kind of Carnival in itself, as men elbow past women to try on secondhand dresses. If you haven't decided on a costume, rummaging through these bins is a good way to brainstorm. The higher-priced **Mardi Gras Center** (tel 504/524–4384; 831 Chartres St., French Quarter) is a nice French Quarter shop located near Jackson Square that can supply you with no-fuss, ready-to-wear costumes. All the classic themes are represented here, from belly dancers to gorillas to contemporary politicians. On a weekend prior to Mardi Gras, the French Market holds an annual **Mardi Gras Mask Market** (tel 504/522–2621) at the Mississippi River between Ursulines and Dumaine streets. Many of the old-style masks for sale are quite stunning, with abstract shapes or animal heads created from feathers, leather, or papier-mâché.

To bead or not to bead... Parade-goers fall into two general categories: those who bead and those who don't. If you're a "beader," you're running up to the floats, waving your arms, and shouting, "Throw me something, Mister." If not, you're hanging back, enjoying the marching bands and offering adroit comments on the floats' artistic flourishes. Beaders come from all walks of life: well-heeled ladies and gents sport delicate pink and purple beads, while burly guys in tank tops swagger down the street wearing long bead strands doubled over Rambo-style.

During Mardi Gras weekend in the French Quarter, beads are used for bartering in a sort of sexual marketplace. This is the scene that Mardi Gras is becoming famous for: men on streets offering beads, and women in balconies flashing for them. Other times, the men are in balconies, and the flashers are in the streets. Or the roles may be completely reversed, and the women are holding the beads. It all makes for a strange mating ritual that would cause Dr. Ruth's head to spin. (Warning: police are much more likely to run men into central lockup for indecent exposure than they are to arrest women.) If you want to start your night with a full bank of beads, **Mid-City's Accent Annex** (tel 504/821–8885 or 800/322–2368; 1120 S. Jefferson Davis Pkwy., Mid-City) sells all varieties by the gross, at prices much lower than what the French Quarter shops are asking.

Top ten secrets on how to catch beads in a parade... Although flashing for beads in parades is becoming more common, an unwritten rule says to leave this activity for the French Quarter—after all, parades are still considered a family event in New Orleans. The following methods for attracting beads, however, are perfectly acceptable: 1) Hold a baby (or stand next to one); 2) Stand next to a group of nuns; 3) Watch the parades in residential neighborhoods, instead of overcrowded Canal Street; 4) If you hear someone near you yelling out the first name of a friend who's on a float, start yelling that name, too; 5) Be specific. Ask, "Mister, could I please have those yellow and green clown face long beads?"; 6) Offer to trade a can of beer or a basket of Popeye's fried chicken; 7) Give 'em a target: lift up your hat or some other kind of basket; 8) Tell 'em it's your first Mardi Gras; 9) When the beads fall on the ground, step on them before you pick them up. (If they fall in a gutter on Canal Street, though, let them go); and 10) A local favorite: tell 'em the beads are for your poor, sick mama at home. Be convincing.

Biggest night parades... You have to get up early for the best Mardi Gras parades. **Zulu**, which hits the streets Carnival Day (Tuesday) at 8:30am, features the city's most prized parade throw, the hand-painted Zulu coconut. **Rex** rolls immediately behind Zulu; it's the vehicle for the King of Carnival himself. But two of the season's biggest processions hit the streets at dusk. The Saturday before Mardi Gras, **Endymion** rolls through Mid-City and down Canal Street to the CBD. This parade is known for its extra-long "super floats" and a great selection of marching bands. Another giant parade is **Bacchus**, which rolls through Uptown and down St. Charles Avenue on Sunday night. The first parade to have a national celebrity as grand marshal, Bacchus is perhaps best known for its really tall "King Kong," "Mamma Kong," and "Baby Kong" floats, which usually get hung up on some low-hanging telephone wire and slow the parade down for hours.

The best night parade... The **Krewe Du Vieux** parade has no giant super floats, national celebrities, or massive throws of beads: Instead, it sports clever satire, goofy throws, and real local spirit. That's why this is the one parade that locals—even those who don't go to any other parades—always attend. It all began in 1979, when a group of 50 artists dressed up like cockroaches and paraded around the Contemporary Arts Center. Past kings have included chef Paul Prudhomme (who rode in a giant gumbo pot), stripper GiO (who waved a dildo scepter), and beloved jazzman Danny Barker. Instead of beads, expect throws of condoms, plastic doggy-do, and duct tape (from people dressed like ducks). Unlike the larger parades, this one starts in the Faubourg Marigny and marches right through the French Quarter. The very popular Krewe Du Vieux Doo ball at the end of the parade is open to the public, and always includes a brass band jam, along with a hot local dance band, such as the Iguanas. Krewe Du Vieux parades on a Saturday evening, usually two to three weeks before Mardi Gras. Check local media for details or call 504/943–7970.

Where the locals put on their costumes... Due to the massive crowds, costumers rarely travel on Bourbon Street. If you want to see the best outfits, wander the more residential **lower French Quarter** (near Esplanade Avenue). At noon each Mardi Gras, the Bourbon Street Awards brings the best transvestite maskers to the blocks near the **intersection of Bourbon and Orleans streets**, and these folks stay in this area through the evening.

Costumers of all varieties usually congregate in **Jackson Square**, where they wind up engaging in debating matches with crowds of religious evangelists. Go figure. The twenty- and thirtysomething hipster crowd meets on **Frenchmen Street** in the Faubourg Marigny.

Where the tourists take off their costumes... If you want to start a Mardi Gras amateur strip show, all you need is a balcony. There's just something about the distance between street people and balcony people that promotes all kinds of situations that wouldn't develop face-to-face. "Show your (add name of body part here)" has become a Mardi Gras rallying cry, and MTV and other outlets have carried this motto to the masses (it even showed up at the Woodstock anniversary). How do you become a balcony person? First, you can rent a balcony room in a Bourbon Street hotel; **The Inn** on Bourbon (tel 504/524–7611; 541 Bourbon St.) has 32 of them. A cheaper route is to pay a few bucks and get on the balcony at any bar or restaurant on the strip. Here are some other important facts to know: on Bourbon Street, geography is marked by sexual preference. From a district that starts roughly with the balcony at **Maiden Voyage** (tel 504/524–0010; 225 Bourbon St.) and continues to the one at the **Cat's Meow** (tel 504/523–1157; 701 Bourbon St.), the scene is exclusively straight. On the 800 and 900 blocks of Bourbon, the balconies of the *Parade* (tel 504/529–2107; 801 Bourbon St.), **Oz** (tel 504/593–9491; 800 Bourbon St.), and **Café Lafitte in Exile** (tel 504/522–8397; 901 Bourbon St.) are just as exclusively filled with gay men. In other words, what gets you beads on one end of Bourbon Street won't even get you a second look on the other.

Mardi Gras balls you can attend... For old-line bashes, it's not what you know, and it's not who you know: it's who the person you know knows. Most Mardi Gras balls are secretive, elite events, and invitations are not available to the general public. This exclusivity is considered part of the tradition. When some political leaders tried to pass legislation to require parade "krewes" to open their membership to such local groups as blacks and Jews, several old-line parades took their floats and went home. They still haven't returned to the streets. However, a number of new groups now have their post-parade balls open to the average Joe and Josephine. The price of a ticket gets you inside the building where the floats conclude their journey, and riders usually save their biggest throws for this grand finale. The ball also includes food and live music.

On the Saturday before Mardi Gras, the **Krewe of Tucks** ends its parade with the giant Party Gras (tel 504/837–1310 or 504/523–1227, or Ticketmaster at 504/522–5555 or 800/488–5252). Started by a group of Loyola college students in 1969, Tucks is a rollicking parade with a good sense of humor, and its ball is a lot of fun. The big news in 1994 was when singer Harry Connick, Jr., started a new Lundi Gras parade, the **Krewe of Orpheus**. Named after the Greek muse Calliope, this huge parade honors traditional New Orleans jazz and R&B. Local musicians ride the floats, and riders toss doubloons with the imprints of Professor Longhair, Sweet Emma, and other music legends. Immediately following that annual parade is the giant **Orpheuscapade** (tel 504/822–7211 or 504/822–7200), another ball that's open to the public.

Where to go on Lundi Gras... The "official" **Lundi Gras show at the Spanish Plaza** at Riverwalk (tel 504/522–1555) is very touristy, and the whole affair smacks too much of civic promotion. (You can just imagine the suits in a meeting: "We have all these people in town. If we can get them near the shopping mall....") The event starts with music by big local acts, including a headliner, such as Dr. John or Cowboy Mouth. The King of Rex arrives via the Mississippi River and is greeted by the Mayor of New Orleans, and the whole deal winds up with a big fireworks display.

A much funkier annual tradition can be found at a small Uptown bar called the **Snake and Jake Christmas Club Lounge** (tel 504/861–2802; 7612 Oak St., Uptown): the "Dudfest," an amusing evening reserved for bands that couldn't get any other jobs for Mardi Gras. Other big Monday events are the **Krewe of Orpheus parade** that rolls down St. Charles Avenue, and the mob scene on Bourbon Street.

Cajun Mardi Gras... A day trip into the bayous, prairies, and sugarcane fields of west Louisiana will show you a very different side of Carnival. There are no big floats out here, and you can be sure that nobody wants you to throw beads at them. Instead, Cajuns go on traditional horseback rides called **courirs**, or **Mardi Gras runs**. Here's how it works: costumed riders gather in the morning. A trailer is filled with musicians playing a song called "La danse de Mardi Gras." All day, the riders traverse country roads, visiting farmhouses, where they sing and dance in exchange for some vegetables, rice, money, or a live chicken. (Everyone hopes it's going to be a chicken, because then the riders get to engage in a raucous chase for the bird.) At the end of the day, the ingredients are brought back to the community for a giant gumbo, and everyone eats and dances until they drop. The most popular run is on Fat Tuesday in the small town of **Mamou**, which swells in size with a crowd of tourists, especially regional college students. Other towns have smaller runs on the Sunday before Mardi Gras. Call the **Lafayette Convention and Visitors Commission** (tel 318/232–3808 or 800/346–1958) for a list of Mardi Gras runs.

In search of Mardi Gras Indians... Every year at Mardi Gras, groups of African-American men step out into the streets wearing ornate Indian headdresses and costumes, chanting traditional songs with meanings that few outsiders know. Some of these songs—such as "Hey Pocky Way" and "Iko Iko"—became famous when they were recorded by the Neville Brothers and the Grateful Dead. The Indians aren't just another typical group of Mardi Gras revellers: it's not unusual for the "Big Chief" to spend the entire year hand-sewing his costume, and hundreds or thousands of dollars go into each "new suit." Mardi Gras Indian costumes have been recognized as important African-American folk artifacts, and are exhibited in museums around the world. Still, the best way to see them is in action, moving along the street to the relentless sound of drums and song. On **Mardi Gras**, gangs of Indians circulate around the intersection of Orleans and Claiborne avenues. During **Mardi Gras season**, some tribes perform in music clubs throughout the city: check the listings for the "Wild Magnolias," whose Big Chief Bo Dollis sings like a feathered James Brown. In addition to Mardi Gras, the Indians hit the streets on **St. Joseph's Night** (March 19) and **Super Sunday**

(another Sunday in March; the exact date is hard to predict). The Indians can also be seen and heard on stage at **Jazz Fest**.

The best club scenes during Jazz Fest... Jazz Fest season provides some of the most exciting club-crawling nights of the year. It's not uncommon for local and national music celebs to hop onstage for unannounced jam sessions. The only way to know who is playing where is to keep your ears open for the latest rumor (which may turn out to be just a rumor).

Fittingly, all the jazz clubs are hopping during Jazz Fest. The French Quarter clubs **Donna's Bar & Grill** (tel 504/596–6914; 800 N. Rampart St.), **Funky Butt** (tel 504/558–0872; 714 N. Rampart St.), and the **New Showcase Lounge**, out in Gentilly, (tel 504/945–5612; 1915 N. Broad St.) are all known for seasonal jazz jam sessions that don't let up until 3am or later.

Even if you're not in the mood for paying another cover charge and hearing another band, you can join other Jazz Festers by hanging out in front of the music clubs all night. A college-age crowd packs the neutral ground Uptown next to **Tipitina's** (tel 504/895–8477; 501 Napoleon Ave.) Perhaps the biggest throng fills Frenchmen Street in the Faubourg Marigny in front of **Cafe Brasil** (tel 504/947–9386; 100 Chartres St.). A mellow, local crowd congregates near the **Mermaid Lounge** (tel 504/524–4747; 1102 Constance St.), located on a loiterer-friendly dead-end street in the Warehouse District. Also in the Warehouse District, the **Howlin' Wolf** (tel 504/523–2551; 828 S. Peters St.) has a lively standing-room-only sidewalk scene.

The big tow... Rex may reign on Mardi Gras, but the city's public works parking division wields the real power. Tow trucks work fast and furious during Mardi Gras season; after all, one misparked car can hold up a whole parade. Among the most enforced rules: parking is prohibited along a parade route for two hours before and after the event. Also, parking on neutral grounds—the grassy section in the center of major streets—is prohibited. But the newest parking law is a big one: No on-street parking in the French Quarter. (Check with your hotel to find out what off-street parking is available.) Temporary signs are usually posted with this parking information, but these are occasionally taken down as souvenirs. If you have any doubts, find a parking lot. And if you come back to your car and it isn't there, you can retrieve it at the **impound lot** (tel 504/565–7450; 400 N. Claiborne Ave., Treme). It'll cost you at least $90 to get your car back; MasterCard and Visa are willingly accepted.

During Mardi Gras and Jazz Fest, some enterprising Orleanians erect little parking lots of their own. Folks who live near parade routes during Mardi Gras or near the Fair Grounds during Jazz Fest set up garbage cans or wooden barricades in the streets in front of their homes. Of course they don't own the streets, but if you try to park, the folks will either yell at you or offer to watch your car for a fee— usually about $5. Of course, you could just move the cans, park, and walk away. But this procedure is only advisable if, say, you're in a rental car and you purchased full insurance. (Remember that you won't be there, but the car and the indignant resident will.) Also during Mardi Gras and Jazz Fest, locals will sell parking space on their front lawns or in church lots, usually for $5–10. This is a more legit affair, and it may be the best parking you'll find.

the

arts

4

"I came here sort of like a migratory bird, I guess," Tennessee Williams once said of New Orleans, "going to a more congenial climate." Today, the works of this great American playwright (and former French Quarter resident) are affixed to this town like a rose tattoo. Every day, tourists peer down the tracks in vain for a streetcar named Desire, and if you walk through the Quarter at night, it's a good bet you'll see at least one inspired drunk wobble under a balcony and shout, "Stel-l-l-la!"

Alas, the climate for the arts in New Orleans is somewhat less congenial. Economics play a role: the state legislature flirts with doing away with arts funding altogether, and there are few Big Daddies around to foot the bill. But many locals believe that the real reason for the ill health of the high arts may be the voracious health of the low arts. In New Orleans, common life is enjoyed with an uncommonly dramatic flair—so why drop twelve bucks to spend the evening in a black-box theater? Indeed, when a comedy or drama does become a hit in this town, it's usually because it successfully re-creates the city's mise-en-scène on the small stage. In New Orleans, art is a mirror, not a window.

Folks don't really come to this town to go to the theater or symphony. Still, it's worth taking a look at the *Gambit Weekly* or the Friday "Lagniappe" section of the *Times-Picayune* to check out what's on the boards. Small-scale productions at Zeitgeist or the Contemporary Arts Center have the welcome rough edge of experimentation. Shakespeare in the Park (City Park, that is) and the Saenger's Broadway series can provide a slice of the Big Apple in the Big Easy. And there's nothing quite like seeing a Tennessee Williams classic at Le Petit Théâtre, then stepping into a misty French Quarter night. All together now: "Stel-l-l-la!"

Getting Tickets

Call **Ticketmaster** (tel 504-522–5555 or 800/488–5252) to order tickets by phone for many music, dance, and theater performances, usually for a higher service charge. If you want to save some money, try calling the venues first. Call as far in advance as possible, though few shows are ever sold out.

Where to see Broadway shows... Thanks to a multi-million-dollar facelift, the **Saenger Performing Arts Center** is one of the most attractive grand old theaters in the South. Broadway touring shows regularly touch down here, usually with great success, though there have been a few bumps in the road: in 1995, a giant, city-wide flood seeped into the Saenger, and the costumes for *Fiddler on the Roof* were soaked. But that same year, the Saenger provided the city with its biggest box-office hit ever: the Broadway tour of *The Phantom of the Opera*, which scared up $7 million over a seven-week engagement. Other recent highlights have included Jerry Lewis in *Damn Yankees*. Season subscribers have first shot at tickets, and it's advisable to order tickets in advance. Most seats are good, but the sound quality is affected on the floor seats beneath the balcony.

Home-grown theater... Set in an old Spanish colonial building on the other side of St. Peter Street from Jackson Square, **Le Petit Théâtre du Vieux Carré** has a few stories of its own to tell. Dating to 1797, this structure was once the home of the first Catholic bishop of Louisiana, and also housed the region's last Spanish governor. The interior is nicely preserved, and the courtyard is classic Quarter. With all this graciousness, it's not surprising that Le Petit's fare appeals to traditional tastes, mostly light-hearted musicals and classics. These aren't world-class productions, but they're usually quite enjoyable—especially in these surroundings. This is also the home theater of the annual Tennessee Williams festival. Although the **Southern Repertory Theatre** couldn't be more different in appearance from Le Petit, its theatrical offerings aren't that dissimilar. This nondescript modern facility is lodged on the third floor of the upscale Canal Place shopping mall, just down the hall from a multiplex cinema. The only Equity theater in town, Southern Rep's mission is to explore the Southern mystique, which it does by staging classics by Lillian Hellman, Tennessee, et al, as well as new works by artistic director Rosary O'Neill and others. Other top venues include Kenner's new **Rivertown Repertory Theatre**, which was launched in 1995 with an ambitious and successful production of the *Will Rogers Follies*. Local original works play on **True Brew**'s three-quarter arena stage, nestled in the back of a cozy coffee-house in the Warehouse District. Most works are main-stream comedies, often with a local bent. Out-of-town theater-lovers shouldn't get their hopes up too high.

Southern Rep is New Orleans' only real repertory theater; other companies rove from venue to venue, so you have to scan the theater listings to see who is play-ing where. Some of the city's liveliest work is produced by **Junebug Productions**, an African-American com-pany headed by a superb performer named John O'Neal, who cut his teeth on the legendary politicized theater company Free Southern Theater, a New Orleans–based company that staged adventurous work throughout the South during the Civil Rights era. Emphasizing all aspects of storytelling, Junebug stages productions that range from full-length works to theatrical revues of sto-ries, music, dance, and puppetry. Look out for **Dog and Pony**, responsible for Shakespeare in the Park among other good productions, and Baton Rouge's **Swine Palace**, best known for an outstanding adaptation of *A Confederacy of Dunces* and the Huey Long bioplay *Kingfish*. And Tulane Summer Lyric Theater offers the city's slickest stagings of mainstream musicals. This is the best place in town for song and dance.

Experimental theater, performance art, and spoken word... Folks in local theater circles fre-quently blame the **Contemporary Arts Center** for all that's wrong with experimental theater in New Orleans. Once a pioneer in new works, the CAC seems more comfortable these days to present kitschy plays about child stars and seventies pop culture. Still, the CAC does have its moments: in 1995, playwright Edward Albee came here to direct one of his own works, using an all-local cast. The CAC also co-produces plays by providing a professional venue for some of the best local artists and companies: Junebug frequently presents shows here, and local performance artist Kathy Randels' solo work *Rage Within/Without* provided some of the brightest moments in recent local theater history. Other edgy work can be seen at **Zeitgeist Theatre Experiments**, located in a large downtown warehouse. The result of a heroic effort by founder Rene Broussard, Zeitgeist is the city's only full-time location for cutting edge work, which can be either thrilling or dreadful. **Theatre Marigny**, which has been around since the early eighties, does a decent job with both new works and classics, often with a twist of gender roles: they did *The Boys in the Band* with a female cast, and even reversed the sexes in a stage production of *The Honeymooners.*

Alas, in a town of poets and storytellers, there are few consistent venues for spoken word performances. Local bookshops sponsor occasional readings, which are listed in the Sunday book section of the *Times-Picayune*, and every Sunday at 3pm, the **Maple Leaf Club** hosts live poetry readings. One beloved local scribe, John Sinclair, performs in clubs around town, backed by a band he calls the Blues Scholars—check club listings for details.

Where there's a Will... The productions aren't as polished as those in New York, but **Shakespeare in the Park** always draws a big local crowd that's happy to spend a late spring evening with the great Bard in the great outdoors. As the sun sets over City Park's lagoons, a good cast starts spouting Elizabethan in the comedy or tragedy *du soir*. To make the most of the outdoor setting, the director often finds a way to bring live animals into the play (a horse in *Richard III*, geese in *Taming of the Shrew*). Attendees usually make an evening of it by showing up early with a picnic dinner and a bottle of wine. Seating is on wooden bleachers. Also in the summer, the **Tulane Summer Shakespeare Festival** alternates two plays each season in the university's Lupin Theater. Arrive early to this one, too: Renaissance Festival–style jugglers and entertainers perform on the lawn outside the theater.

Classical sounds... Classical music fans still recall the night when the **Louisiana Philharmonic Orchestra**, in

NEW ORLEANS & THE ARTS

financial collapse, performed *Haydn's Farewell Symphony* and sadly marched one by one off the stage. But that wasn't the last chapter. The LPO restructured itself as a musician-owned symphony, serving as inspiration to monetarily-strapped orchestras throughout the country, and it continues to build steam: in 1995, the new orchestra's first music conductor, Klauspeter Seibel, came on board. Some of the most attended performances are the Beethoven and Blue Jeans concerts, where you can listen to Ludwig in clothes you couldn't wear to Galatoire's. Other venues for classical music include free Sunday evening performances at two Uptown churches: **Christ Church Cathedral** on St. Charles Avenue and **Episcopal** on Jackson Avenue.

What's opera, doc?... Opera recently celebrated its bicentennial in New Orleans; the May 22, 1796 performance of *Sylvain* at the old **Theatre St. Pierre** was the first full-scale opera production in the United States. And in the mid-nineteenth century, the French Opera House, at the corner of Bourbon and Toulouse streets, was all the rage in New Orleans high society. A plaque is all that remains of that landmark, but opera still has its local audience. The **New Orleans Opera Association** consistently produces sell-out shows in the ornate **Mahalia Jackson Theatre of the Performing Arts**, located in Armstrong Park near the French Quarter. In 1995, the Jefferson Performing Arts Society also entered the opera fray with two traditional productions staged at the **Jefferson Performing Arts Center** in Metairie. **The Loyola College of Music** has also drawn rave notices for its work with new Loyola music faculty member David Morelock.

Men in tights... Most of the good stuff comes from the road. The **New Orleans Ballet Association** has wonderfully eclectic tastes when booking touring dance companies to play New Orleans, and has brought everyone from Japan's Sakai Juku to Bill T. Jones to Moses Pendleton's Momix. All performances are in the lavish **Mahalia Jackson Theatre of the Performing Arts** in Armstrong Park. The Jefferson Performing Arts Society also books touring outfits that play the Jefferson Performing Arts Center. The most active groups on the local scene are ethnic dance companies; Komenka Ethnic Dance

Ensemble, Kumbuka African Drum & Dance Collective, and N'Kafu Cultural African Dance Company perform at festivals and various theaters throughout the year. Finally, keep an eye out for the local **Lula Elzy Dance Theatre**, a great modern dance company that occasionally plays the **Orpheum Theatre**.

Culture for kids... If you have kids in tow, you have a few options besides plunking them in a video arcade with a roll of quarters. **Le Petit Théâtre du Vieux Carré**'s weekend children's series, called Teddy's Corner, is very popular with local families. In the summer, Tulane University's **Patchwork Players** offers new adaptations of fairy tales, such as *Hansel and Gretel*. (The emphasis is on audience participation, so everyone should get a turn in the oven.) And the **Louisiana Philharmonic Orchestra** gets in the act with its Family Discovery series. The LPO even has the chutzpah to compete with Disney: one recent offering was *Aladdin* presented in a team effort with a local ballet troupe.

Those big, big rock shows... When those dinosaur rock acts with names like Paul McCartney, the Eagles, and the Rolling Stones lumber into town, they play the **Superdome**, a massive concrete mushroom of a building that occupies 52 acres of downtown New Orleans. When not a rock hall, the Dome is home field to the Saints football team and various trade shows, as well as the annual Essence Festival of contemporary African-American music. Most other big touring acts—especially alternative rock shows—choose the **Lakefront Arena** on the campus of the University of New Orleans. Security is fairly lax here: the air can be thick with marijuana haze following some shows. General admission seating is divided into upper and lower levels; the floor becomes a big, beer-slick mosh pit that provides good mileage for crowd surfers. (Probably the town's grandest mosh of all was for Nirvana, which played a memorable show at the Lakefront the year before Kurt Cobain's death.) Recent shows have included multiple nights by Pearl Jam, whose series of shows gained some notoriety after lead singer Eddie Vedder became involved in a French Quarter brawl.

Two grand, historic theaters sit on the opposite sides of Canal Street, where they look like before/after photos.

The **State Palace Theater** is in complete disrepair, with torn curtains, worn carpet, threadbare velvet seat cushions, and the musty smell of faded grandeur; the front seats have been removed to enlarge the dance space. It plays host to rap and alternative bands, along with hip old acts like Elvis Costello. Across the street, the **Saenger Performing Arts Center** has been lovingly restored, right down to the seat cushions and right up to the beautiful *faux* constellations that light up the ceiling. Many nights are reserved for touring Broadway plays, but the Saenger stage has also seen rockers such as Bruce Springsteen (on his acoustic tour). The security at Saenger is strict: any dancing will be conducted while remaining seated, and any flames will be quickly extinguished.

The best movie screens... Like every town, New Orleans has its share of shoebox movie theaters located in shopping malls. But for a really big screen, go to **Lakeside Theatre**—this old house may be a little run-down, but at least it feels like a movie theater. Don't confuse it with **Lakeside Cinema**, which is located across the street in Lakeside Shopping Center. (By the way, there's not a lake in sight.) The best mall theater by far is the **AMC Galleria**, which offers eight screens in a silvery futuristic mall that nobody ever goes to except to go to the movies. Every room in the Galleria has a large screen and superior sound. If you're Downtown or in the French Quarter, the **Canal Place Cinema** is within walking distance; located on the third floor of the Canal Place mall, it even offers free validated parking. It usually screens a mix of Hollywood and foreign/independent movies, and is the site of the New Orleans Film and Video Festival. There's only one problem with Canal Place: most of the rooms are tiny, one of them is perpetually out-of-focus, and another one stinks. Literally. If the movie isn't showing in the one nice theater (the largest, "main" room), you might want to think twice.

Best place to read subtitles... For foreign and alternative cinema, the grandest theater in town is the **Prytania**, which is located in a residential Uptown neighborhood. Unfortunately, its programming has become lackluster in recent years, throwing it into disfavor with local film buffs. Ditto for **Canal Place Cinema**, which frequently relegates its revivals, independents, and foreign films to the small rooms while a Hollywood blockbuster plays the larger theater. For the best variety of movies, there are two places in town that are as alternative as the movies they show. **Movie Pitchers** is rather dingy, has fairly poor sound and picture quality, and is a true local favorite. Get there early to snare one of the couches; the seats in the back aren't very comfortable. Movie Pitchers gets its name from its beer and wine menu, and it also serves sandwiches, which you can order before the movie and have (quietly) brought to your seat. **Zeitgeist Theatre Experiments** frequently shows films that wouldn't find a screen anywhere else in town, including work by local filmmakers. With plastic molded seats and a feeble air-conditioner, this isn't all that comfortable either—but good art rarely is, right? One more thing: Zeitgeist's gay films are often porn, so you may want to call first for a description.

The Index

AMC Galleria. This eight-screen mall cinema has the best sound and the largest pictures.... *Tel 504/838–8309. 1 Galleria Blvd., Metairie.*

Canal Place Cinema. This is one of the city's crummiest theaters, but it screens some of the best movies, and hosts the annual New Orleans Film and Video Festival.... *Tel 504/581–5400. 333 Canal St., Downtown.*

Christ Church Cathedral. This striking St. Charles Avenue church presents occasional Sunday afternoon classical concerts.... *Tel 504/895–6602. 2919 St. Charles Ave., Uptown.*

Contemporary Arts Center. In two modern, well-equipped theaters, a varied lineup of performers and companies do work that can be as experimental as New Orleans gets.... *Tel 504/523–1216 or 504/528–3800. 900 Camp St., Warehouse District.*

Dog and Pony. One of the city's best theater companies stages works in various locations, and in May offers two Shakespeare plays in City Park.... *Tel 504/897–2466. P.O. Box 71602, New Orleans, 70172.*

Jefferson Performing Arts Center. This is the theater for the Jefferson Performing Arts Society, an active organization that stages touring and local theater, opera, dance, and popular music.... *Tel 504/885–2000. East Jefferson High School, 400 Phlox Ave., Metairie.*

Junebug Productions. This popular African-American theater company stages works in a variety of venues, including the CAC.... *Tel 504/524–8257. P.O. Box 2331, New Orleans, 70176.*

Lakefront Arena. Located near Lake Pontchartrain, this is the arena of choice for many touring rock bands.... *Tel 504/286–7222. For most shows, call Ticketmaster at 504/522–5555. University of New Orleans, 6801 Franklin Ave., Lakefront.*

Lakeside Theatre. If you want to avoid the mall multi-plexes, check out this old cinema with really big screens.... *Tel 504/888–5300. 3526 Veterans Memorial Blvd., Metairie.*

Le Petit Théâtre du Vieux Carré. Billed as the oldest continuously running community theater—or something like that—this attractive complex is located near Jackson Square. In addition to the regular season, it's the home of the annual Tennessee Williams festival and a popular children's series.... *Tel 504/522–2081 or 504/522–9958. 616 St. Peter St., French Quarter.*

Louisiana Philharmonic Orchestra. This member-run orchestra presents about 50 concerts in the Orpheum Theatre each season, including the perennial favorite, Beethoven and Blue Jeans.... *Tel 504/523–6530. Orpheum Theater, 129 University Pl., Downtown.*

Mahalia Jackson Theatre of the Performing Arts. Luckily, this gorgeous theater is one building in Armstrong Park that Harrah's Casino didn't take over.... *Tel 504/565–7470. 801 N. Rampart St., Treme.*

The Maple Leaf Club. Sunday afternoons in this popular music bar are given over to live poetry readings.... *Tel 504/866–9359. 8316 Oak St., Uptown.*

Movie Pitchers. This collection of small screening rooms also presents live comedy and plays, especially one acts.... *Tel 504/488–8881. 3941 Bienville St., Mid-City.*

New Orleans Ballet Association. This organization brings in a variety of marquee names in the world of dance, from avant-garde to classical. All performances are in the Mahalia Jackson Theatre for the Performing Arts.... *Tel 504/522–0996. 639 Loyola Ave., Downtown.*

New Orleans Opera Association. This organization keeps the New Orleans opera tradition alive by annually staging two well-received productions at the Mahalia Jackson Theatre for the Performing Arts.... *Tel 504/529–2278. 333 St. Charles Ave., Downtown.*

Orpheum Theatre. Matched in beauty only by the Mahalia Jackson and the Saenger, this is one of the city's grand old theaters. The Louisiana Philharmonic Orchestra performs here.... *Tel 504/524–3285. 129 University Place, Downtown.*

Patchwork Players. This summer children's theater series stages original adaptations of classic stories.... *Tel 504/865–5105. Rogers Memorial Chapel, Tulane University, Uptown.*

Prytania Theatre. This attractive, slightly dank cinema offers both mainstream and art-house fare.... *Tel 504/895–4513. 5339 Prytania St., Uptown.*

Rivertown Repertory Theatre. This comfortable suburban theater is one of the newest in the area; mainstream musicals and dramas are on tap here.... *Tel 504/468–7221. 419 Minor St., Kenner.*

Roussel Hall. This austere but acoustically superb theater at Loyola University has been used for everything from opera to the chamber music supergroup Kronos Quartet.... *Tel 504/865–3037. Loyola University, Uptown.*

Saenger Performing Arts Center. This completely refurbished historic downtown theater is New Orleans' most attractive music and theater venue, and is used for Broadway touring companies. Don't forget to count the stars in the ceiling.... *Tel 504/524–2490. 143 N. Rampart St., Downtown. Ticket prices vary.*

Shakespeare in the Park. This outdoor series of Shakespearean productions is held each May in City Park.... *Tel 504/483–9376. 1 Palm Dr., Mid-City.*

Southern Repertory Theatre. This comfortable theater, home to New Orleans' only Equity company, specializes in Southern playwrights. The venue doubles as a screening room during the New Orleans Film and Video Festival.... *Tel 504/861–8163. Canal Pl., Downtown.*

State Palace Theatre. This run-down old theater is home to touring alternative rock and rap acts.... *Tel 504/522–4435. 1108 Canal St., Downtown.*

Superdome. In addition to football games and trade shows, this giant indoor stadium is home to engorged rock acts and the Essence Festival.... *Tel 504/587–3663. Sugar Bowl Dr., New Orleans.*

Swine Palace Productions. This excellent Baton Rouge company usually brings its best works to New Orleans, including a memorable production of *A Confederacy of Dunces.* Look for great work by local actor and Roseanne cast member John "Spud" McConnell.... *Tel 504/388–3527. Louisiana State University, Baton Rouge.*

Theatre Marigny. This mainstay in the local arts community is a bit more adventurous than most local theaters.... *Tel 504/944–2653. 616 Frenchmen St., Faubourg Marigny.*

Trinity Episcopal Church. The Trinity Artist series presents free classical and jazz concerts here on Sunday evenings.... *Tel 504/522–0276. 1329 Jackson Ave., Uptown.*

True Brew. Original productions (mostly comedies) play in a small theater in the back of this coffeehouse. Don't be confused: there's another True Brew in the Bayou St. John region that doesn't have a theater.... *Tel 504/522–2907. 200 Julia St., Warehouse District.*

Tulane Summer Lyric Theater. This series of quality musicals is the most popular of the summer Tulane theater events.... *Tel 504/865–5269. Dixon Hall, Tulane University, Uptown.*

Tulane Summer Shakespeare Festival. Two of the Bard's plays run on alternate nights, and special performances feature discount prices, as well as guest lectures by Tulane faculty.... *Tel 504/865–5106. Lupin Theater, Tulane University, Uptown.*

Zeitgeist Theatre Experiments. A seat-of-the-pants operation, this large warehouse space is the city's only full-time center devoted exclusively to avant-garde theater, film, music, and visual arts.... *Tel 504/524–0064. 740 O'Keefe Ave., Downtown.*

spo

rts 5

If you must see the sorry
state of professional sports
in New Orleans, take a trip
to the Superdome during
the final quarter of a
Saints game. Look up in
the stands. See the people

with bags over their heads? Those are the fans.

Year after year, the town's only pro sports franchise turns in a woeful record. There was a long stretch when the Saints didn't have a prayer of making the postseason; then there were several years when they earned a wild-card bid to the playoffs—no matter, the franchise has still yet to win a play-off game. Nevertheless, at the start of each new season, fans are back at the Dome, ready to cheer for their team. Every fall, the Saints unveil a newer, dopier slogan, such as "Here to Win" or "We Believe." But by the end of the season, the bag-heads (also called "The Ain'ts") invariably return, as predictable as swallows in Capistrano.

Louisiana's license plates advertise the state as a "Sportsman's Paradise," referring to the miles of wetlands and waterways that make for happy hunting and fishing grounds. But in the arena of professional spectator sports, New Orleans is a Sportsman's Purgatory. And it's not just football. Folks here remember a recent doomed attempt to lure a pro basketball team to the city, when the owners of the Minnesota Timberwolves indicated that they were hot to re-settle the team in the Big Easy. (The improbable moniker "Louisiana Timberwolves" didn't seem to bother anybody.) In the full court press of civic excitement, the *Times-Picayune* ran a Timberwolves jersey on a full-color, front-page special edition, with the headline, "Got 'Em!" That headline now ranks in the annals with "Dewey Defeats Truman." The Wolves stayed home. And what did that leave for New Orleans? Football and the Saints. Once again, sports fans were left wearing the bag.

Nonetheless, New Orleans does regularly see some of the country's most exciting athletic competitions. Each New Year's Day, the sweetest college football teams invade the Superdome for the Sugar Bowl; the competing colleges' fren-zied fans display their team colors up and down Bourbon Street, transforming the strip into one long, loud cheerleading contest. The Superdome is also a frequent site for the granddaddy game of them all, the Super Bowl. New Orleans has hosted a national record of seven Super Bowls, and the eighth is scheduled for 1997. Other major competitions in the Dome include occasional Final Four playoffs by top college basketball teams in March (nobody who was in attendance will ever forget the 1982 showdown between George-town and North Carolina, which was capped by a final jump shot by Michael Jordan).

Of course, these major events are sold out long in advance. Hotel rooms are booked to capacity, and tickets are only available from scalpers. For the casual sports fan in town for a few days, a good alternative is to hit the minor leagues. The New Orleans Zephyrs baseball team play in an outdoor park conveniently located near the cooling breezes of Lake Pontchartrain. And the New Orleans Riverboat Gamblers play evening soccer at the Pan-American Stadium in City Park.

In active sports, the local philosophy tends to be "Yeah, but it's kind of hot...." When they do take to the tracks, diamonds, courts, and fields, local athletes usually emphasize a sense of fun over heated rivalry—figuring that summers are heated enough as it is. One local foot race threads from bar to bar, sampling coolants along the way; if you hit the lanes at the popular alley/dance club, Mid-City Lanes, your score may suffer (it's hard to keep your aim straight when you're dancing).

Venues and Tickets

Ticketmaster (tel 800/488–5252 or 504/522–5555) is the one charge-by-phone outlet for advance tickets to most major sporting events down here, including the Saints, the Riverboat Gamblers, and the Zephyrs. Caution: Ticketmaster may tack on higher service charges than what you'll get if you order directly from the sports franchise.

When it's not hosting trade shows, music festivals, and circuses, the **Superdome** (tel 504/587–3800; Sugar Bowl Dr., Downtown) is the home of the New Orleans Saints, the Sugar Bowl, Tulane football, and scores of other major sports events. Located within walking distance of a few downtown hotels and bars, this massive concrete construction has the appearance of either a nuclear power plant, an engorged mushroom, or a spaceship. The seating capacity tops 70,000, which assures that tickets never sell out for regular season games. A game here is a good way to beat the heat: nearly 10,000 tons of air-conditioning keep this room cool on even the hottest days and evenings. Daytime tours are available. The site of the 1992 Olympic Track & Field Trials, **Pan-American Stadium** (tel 504/482–7571; 1 Zachary Taylor Dr., City Park, Mid-City) is a handsome open-air arena located in the cultivated oak tree forest of City Park. This is also the home of the minor league New Orleans Riverboat Gamblers soccer team. The minor league New Orleans Zephyrs and the University of New

Orleans Privateers play baseball at **Privateer Park** (tel 504/286–6100; 6801 Franklin Ave., New Orleans East), an attractive diamond in direct line of the cool breezes of Lake Pontchartrain. General seating is in bleachers; reserved chair-backs are available for a higher price. The Zephyrs have announced plans to move to a new 10,500-capacity ballpark being built on Airline Highway in Metairie, slated to open in 1997, but the completion date on this project has been pushed back in the past, and some Privateer Park fans hope it will be pushed back again.

The Lowdown

Where to watch

Sainted football... Although the National Football League franchise the **New Orleans Saints** (tel 504/522–2600; 1500 Poydras St., Downtown) doesn't enjoy much of a record, the team still has widespread support in the city—at least early in the season. Orleanians stand squarely behind their popular quarterback Jim Everett, statistically the Saints' best-ever. (Former QB Archie Manning also remains a legendary sports figure in this town.) The city is not as enthusiastic about Saints management, which has consistently raised ticket prices without showing much team improvement. Nonetheless, the Saints can be a lot of fun: halftime shows feature some of the best marching bands in the land, and catchy team cheers include the evergreen, "Who dat say dey gonna beat dem Saints." Concessions are the tried and true: the Dome Foam and Dome Dogs are just stadium names for the classic sports meal of beer and hot dogs. Saints ticket prices range from $30 to $37; the best place to purchase tickets is at the Superdome, or by phone through the Saints' ticket office. To listen to the game, tune your radio dial to WWL Newsradio, 870 AM.

College football doesn't really enjoy much of a following in New Orleans, mainly because most fans devote their attention to the popular Louisiana State University Tigers, who play in Baton Rouge, about an hour's drive west of the city. The only college team to regularly play the Superdome is **Tulane University's Green Wave** (tel 504/861–3661; 6823 St. Charles Ave., Uptown), who draw a crowd that seems quite tiny in the huge Dome. Every other year, Tulane and LSU face off in a highly anticipated showdown. On the eve of the match,

Hurricane glasses have been known to fly across tables at Pat O'Brien's in the French Quarter.

Hoop dreams deferred... When the Timberwolves stayed in Minnesota, New Orleans' hoop dreams of attracting an NBA franchise to town were dashed to the ground. Still, the city dreams of one day attracting a team, and plans to snare them with a new arena, which is being planned for a site adjacent to the Superdome. For now, local buckets fans content themselves with the annual college Sugar Bowl Basketball Tournament, which plays the Superdome the week prior to the annual Sugar Bowl football play-off. Other occasional events in the Dome include the Final Fours, along with occasional pre-season pro exhibition games. For college basketball, UNO has a good NCAA Division I Privateers team, which plays in the Lakefront Arena; the Tulane Green Wave plays on campus at the **Fogelman Arena** (tel 504/ 865–5810; Tulane University, Wilson Center, Uptown). Each season, the Green Wave also rolls into the Super-dome for a couple of televised games.

Go to the minors, part I: baseball... For six decades, New Orleans supported a professional baseball team called the Pelicans, which played in a stadium across the street from Mid-City Lanes. That stadium has been razed, though a giant wall mural inside the bowling alley depicts those glory days. Baseball fans had something new to cheer about in 1993, when the AAA baseball team the **New Orleans Zephyrs** (tel 504/282– 6777 or 504/282–7505; P.O. Box 24672, New Orleans, 70184) moved to town. The Zephyrs—a farm team for the Milwaukee Brewers—have quickly won a sizable and enthusiastic following, thanks to their decent record: nobody has to pull a bag over their head at one of these games.

A Zephyrs game is an evening straight out of a Norman Rockwell painting. The loudspeakers might play Fats Domino's "I'm Walkin' to New Orleans" when a player is walked. Kids scurry en masse with their mitts into the parking lot when a ball clears the stands. Players wait around and sign autographs at the end of the game. But best of all is the opportunity to laugh at the hapless audience participant in the "Dizzy Bat Race," which features a poor sap spinning around in a circle and then falling down on his backfield when he attempts to run in a straight line. Now, that's entertainment. The Zephyrs play at breezy Privateer Park on the University of New Orleans campus. Privateer Park's concessions are a lot more varied than what you'll find at a Saints game: in addition to the archetypal peanuts and Cracker Jacks, you can find pizza and specialty drinks from Pat O'Brien's (including the frozen "Zephyr" daiquiri). The merchandise—especially the bright green cloth caps—are very cool. UNO's own baseball team, the **Privateers** (tel 504/ 286–6100; University of New Orleans, New Orleans East) also plays here.

Go to the minors, part II: soccer... Soccer is the metric system of sports—the rest of the world just loves it, which may explain why it will never completely win the heart of our stubborn nation. Nonetheless, the **New Orleans Riverboat Gamblers** (tel 504/244–SCOR, 504/ 482–7571 during game) is a welcome newcomer in town. Started as a provisional team in 1993, the Gamblers are now a farm team for the professional franchise the Dallas Burn, and games attract an average crowd of 1,500 (many from area youth soccer leagues). The season runs from the beginning of April to the middle of August; most matches are held Saturdays at 7:30pm, in the open-air Pan-American Stadium. Though it had been used for football for many years, this stadium was originally designed for soccer, and the front seats are located within a few feet of the field. Seating is in metal bleachers. The air is tolerably cool by evening, but keep in mind that this ain't air-conditioned. As is the case with minor league baseball, these soccer games are low-key and fun, with goofy contests at halftime, and plenty of giveaways each night. At game's end, throngs of kids run onto the field to get players' autographs. Advance tickets are available for four bucks a seat, or at the gate for seven bucks (with a discount for kids).

Off to the races... Due to the extreme heat of New Orleans' summers, the horse racing season at the **Fair Grounds** (tel 504/944–5515; 1751 Gentilly Blvd., New Orleans) is the reverse of what you'll find at tracks in states such as Kentucky: The inaugural race is on Thanksgiving, and the season runs through the middle of

NEW ORLEANS $\bigcirc$ **SPORTS**

April (when the Fair Grounds is quickly transformed into Jazz Fest). This is one of the oldest tracks in the nation, but much of the place's charm went up in smoke when the grandstand was destroyed in a 1993 fire. Permanent replacements have yet to be constructed, and depending on the outcome of state efforts to ban video poker, they may never be. (Video poker machines provide much of the track's revenue.) In recent years, competition from casinos has given the Fair Grounds a run for its money. Still, this is a pleasant place to stop by, sip a bourbon, and shake your program at your chosen pony. On most days, post time is 1pm, but Friday's 3pm post time extends that day's final races into the evening.

Where to play

Shooting pool... Pool sharks can swim into just about any bar in town and find at least one semi-decent table. But the most serious players will want to check out **Racketeers** (tel 504/840–7665; 200 Monticello Ave., Jefferson), open 24 hours. This hall has a seriously shady past as an underground casino. These days, however, everything is on the level (but take the time to ask the bartender about the rough old days). The stark gray building is popular with college students on late weekend nights; 25 regulation tables are up for grabs at $2.50 an hour. There's also a bar, a few foosball tables, a juke box, and video poker machines, but none of these distract the customers from their main reason for being here: to sink the ball in the pocket.

Bowl-a-rama... Let's not be modest about at least one thing: New Orleans has the world's most fun bowling alley. This may also be the best place in the world to bowl with the stars: everyone from Mick Jagger to Tom Cruise has checked out the **Mid-City Lanes** (tel 504/482–3133; 4133 S. Carrollton Ave., Mid-City) for its signature hybrid of music and bowling called Rock 'n' Bowl. In fact, Cruise's shoes are even mounted and displayed in the stairwell entrance. Located in the residential Mid-City neighborhood, this is also one of New Orleans' most popular nightclubs to hear zydeco, blues, and R&B. But day or night, it's also a fully operational, one-of-a-kind bowling alley that dates back to the mid-forties. Week-nights see some league action, but the above-ground ball return and manual scoring (not to mention a crowd of dancers that have been known to jitterbug in the bowling pits) keep this from being a recommended alley for serious competitors. The lanes stay open until about 1 or 2am weeknights, and later on weekends. Rates are by the hour, no matter if you're solo or competing with the entire cast of *Interview With the Vampire.*

Of course, if the thought of people dancing in your bowling lane makes you break out in a cold sweat, skip Mid-City and head out to **Don Carter's All Star Lanes** (tel 504/443–5353; 3640 Williams Blvd., Kenner). The largest alley in town (at least on this side of the river), Carter's has 64 lanes and fully automatic scorers, and has been the site of the Brunswick World Team Challenge. Plus, it's open late: until midnight Monday through Thursday, and until 3am on weekends. League teams tie up the lanes until about 9pm, but after that there's pretty good availability, on a first-come, first-bowl basis. Rates are by the game, per person. Carter's also has a full bar and cafe open during bowling hours, as well as pool tables and a video arcade.

Skate late... The skating scene around here is kids on wheels, for the most part. At **Airline Skate Center** (tel 504/733–2248; 6711 Airline Hwy., Metairie), high-schoolers rock and roll to the latest radio tunes on summer weekends; look for types like Ned Flanders and family on the special Christian music nights. Located in a classic New Orleans blue-collar neighborhood, **Skateland** (tel 504/947–2079; 1019 Charbonnet St., Ninth Ward) has been keeping the wheels in motion for almost a half-century. You have to go across the river for the most grown-up rink, **Westbank Skate Country** (tel 504/392–2227; 1100 Terry Pkwy., Gretna). On Thursdays, the crowd is restricted to 18 or older, and the skating goes till midnight. Otherwise, expect a high-school crowd on weekends.

Volleyball... Located in the middle of downtown's parking lots and office buildings, the **Buffalo Beach Club** (tel 504/595–8986; 867 Magazine St., Downtown) is a sandy oasis. Attached to a rather average-looking bar you'll find

NEW ORLEANS ◡ SPORTS

a regulation size volleyball court complete with eight inches of sand. What's even more strange: many nights, this complete volleyball setup sits empty. Tournament play fills it on some weeknights, especially in the spring. But if you bring enough friends to form a couple of teams, there's a good chance you'll be able to pick the ball up at the bar and spike the night away.

For gym rats... Even if you're not a fitness buff, you may want to fake it for a day, just to visit the swank **New Orleans Athletic Club** (tel 504/525–2375; 222 N. Rampart St., Downtown/French Quarter). Dating to the late nineteenth century, this is the second-oldest health club in the nation; it has been keeping society's cream whipped into shape at this location since 1929. When movies are filming in town, stars like Kevin Costner and Alec Baldwin come here to stay trim. Other personages to perspire here are Clark Gable, Tennessee Williams, and Bob Hope, along with such athletes as Kareem Abdul Jabbar (who gave basketball clinics) and boxer John L. Sullivan (who trained here for the first heavyweight championship fight). Boxing is the classic NOAC activity, but modern innovations include aerobics and state-of-the-art Nautilus equipment, such as recumbent cycles equipped with cable TV. You can hobnob with the city's elite while you play handball and squash; regard the French Quarter while you circle the rooftop track; or pull up a leather armchair for a game of chess in the lounge. Day passes are available for $20; longer visits are also negotiable. The club is open until 10pm weeknights and 6pm weekends.

The best hotel exercise facilities are at the **Hilton's Rivercenter Racquet and Health Club** (tel 504/556–3742; New Orleans Hilton, 2 Poydras St., Downtown). Open until 10:30pm weeknights and 7pm weekends, this club has a membership of 600 locals, and attracts about fifteen thousand out-of-towners each year. It's $10 a visit, with lower rates for Hilton guests. For recreation, Rivercenter has eight indoor and three outdoor tennis courts; four racquetball courts; three squash courts; a 1/4-mile rooftop jogging path; an outdoor basketball half-court; and an indoor golf academy. The weight room has Nautilus New Generation machines and other top-of-the-line devices. The vibe is mainly corporate types trying to stay in shape; no Gold's Gym or Spandex meat markets here. Also good is the **Meridien Sports Center** (tel 504/527–6750; 614 Canal St., Downtown), located at Le Meridien hotel. The fee is $9 daily, and the club is open until 9pm. Finally, there are two YMCAs located in the downtown area; the best is **Lee Circle YMCA** (tel 504/568–9622; 920 St. Charles Ave., Lee Circle). Highlights include a superior pool; an indoor basketball full-court; racquetball courts; a good collection of training machines and free weights; and the price: $5 a day, $2 for Y members. Open until 9pm weeknights, 5pm weekends. Also Downtown, the **Superdome YMCA** (tel 504/568-9622; Superdome, Sugar Bowl Dr., Downtown) is much smaller, with no pool or indoor sports. It is open weekdays until 7pm.

Staying cool in a pool... The one drawback of the Hilton's Rivercenter Racquet and Health Club is that it doesn't include the hotel's fine pool, which is only available for guests. That's not the case at the **Meridien Sports Center** (tel 504/527–6750; 614 Canal St., Downtown), which has a 35-foot outdoor pool located on the hotel's eighth floor, included in the $9 day fee for those who aren't staying at the Meridien. However, serious swimmers will be frustrated here by hotel guests splish-splashing around. Of course, if you want to dive into the lap pool of luxury, there's nothing quite like the marbled accommodations at the **New Orleans Athletic Club** (tel 504/525-2375; 222 N. Rampart St., Downtown/French Quarter), where you'll really be swimming in it, surrounded by white pillars and potted plants. There's a $20 day pass for nonmembers. Things are a little more proletarian at the **Lee Circle YMCA** (tel 504/568–9622; 920 St. Charles Ave., Lee Circle), which has an excellent 20-yard pool; day fee is $5, or $2 for Y members.

The tennis racket... During its heyday in the 1970's, **City Park Tennis Center** (tel 504/483–9383; 1 Palm Dr., City Park, Mid-City) offered the South's largest selection of tennis courts. When the tennis fad subsided, some of these were converted to parking lots, but this is still the city's biggest and best place to hit a few. The 36 courts (21 hard surface and 15 soft) are lighted for play in the evening (which is the only humane time to play summer tennis). The center stays open until 10pm weeknights and 7pm weekends. Racquets are available for rent, and a pro shop sells tennis balls and other equipment. Tip: tickets for courts are available for purchase up to 30 days in advance of play. Evenings are often booked; you're taking a chance if you show up for first-come, first-serve. (That's a pun.) The courts are located on the northwest quadrant of City Park, near the intersection of City Park and Marconi Street. Other night courts (that's another pun) can be found at the **Hilton's Rivercenter Racquet and Health Club** (tel 504/556–3742; New Orleans Hilton, 2 Poydras St., Downtown), which has eight indoor courts and three right outside the club on a sixth-floor rooftop. The Rivercenter charges a $10 day fee.

Jogging along... Running at dark may be faster than walking at dark, but when you're solo, it's no less dangerous. Most of the city's best runs—including the Mississippi levee—should be avoided after sundown. That's why **Southern Runner** (tel 504/899–3333 or 504/891–9999; 6112 Magazine St., Uptown) sponsors frequent night runs, the most infamous being the annual 5K Witch's Moonlight Run, which draws a couple thousand people together on the last Friday in October. The police-escorted race starts at the Superdome and winds through the Downtown to a costumed dance at the Hyatt Regency. There are prizes for the best costume, and plenty of people jog in quite elaborate getups. Other on-foot traditions are a 5K run on the last Friday night in September, to benefit the Louisiana Philharmonic Orchestra. Following the race, the orchestra performs a full, open-air concert. A series of smaller runs are held every other Wednesday night, from April to August, each one with different themes and prizes: there's a progressive, on-foot blackjack game, as well as a crawfish run that features a crawfish race and a complete crawfish feast. All these events adhere to the New Orleans running philosophy: short race, long party.

The **New Orleans Track Club** (tel 504/482–6682; P.O. Box 52003, New Orleans, 70152) also sponsors some evening runs. Good running tracks are available at the **New Orleans Athletic Club** (tel 504/525–2375; 222 N. Rampart St., Downtown/French Quarter)—$20 day pass for non-members; and the **Hilton's Rivercenter**

Racquet and Health Club (tel 504/556–3742; New Orleans Hilton, 2 Poydras St., Downtown)—$10 day pass for non-hotel guests.

Miniature golf... Along the Mississippi Gulf Coast, about an hour to the east of New Orleans, lie some truly surreal miniature golf courses, haunted by giant concrete skeletons and dinosaurs. Unfortunately, that building trend didn't extend into the Crescent City. Occasionally, national chains like Putt-Putt have come to town, but they were driven out by the summer heat. The best minigolf that the city currently has to offer is **Celebration Station** (tel 504/887–7888; 5959 Veterans Memorial Blvd., Metairie), and it's pretty much just for the small fries. Located right off I-10 (and not far enough away to totally escape the noise and exhaust), this outdoor complex also offers a go-cart track, bumper boats, a hundred video games, and batting cages. The crowd gets a little older at night; the station stays open until 9pm on weeknights and 11pm weekends.

Batting cages... Swingers head to **Batter's Box** (tel 504/888–8058; 4021 I-10 Service Rd., Metairie) to work on their form or to take out the frustrations of the day on an innocent little stitched ball. The Box is busiest during the day; there's usually no wait at night for one of seven cages (two for softball). Tokens are a dollar, and each token gets you 14 balls. The folks who come here are serious about batting practice; most of them are in leagues or on school teams. Also available is a circular go-cart track; cars are rented by the half-minute. There's also a game room and snack machines. Other batting cages are available at **Celebration Station** (tel 504/887–7888; 5959 Veterans Memorial Blvd., Metairie).

NEW ORLEANS SPORTS

hangi

ng out

You can clop through the Quarter in a mule-drawn buggy, or scurry past the shadows on a ghost tour. Bargain shop on Bourbon Street to compare the prices of ticky T-shirts and tacky T-shirts. Take a ferry boat to the other side of the river; turn around for the return trip. Yes, you can fill the night with activity.

But this, as they say with raised brows, just really isn't the way it's done here. Long before the word "slacker" defined a generation, it described New Orleans nightlife. The real scene isn't in the club; it's hanging out on the plastic molded chairs and curbsides in front of the club door. Once again, you can blame it on the weather: in that half of the year we call "summer," this is the only humane time to be outdoors. So we delay, and we dally. By fall, it's ingrained. These are the laconic "Southern Nights" that local songwriter Allen Toussaint had in mind.

Orleanians don't really speak with a drawl, but on any given night, we can certainly move with one.

The Lowdown

You can't miss the mules... All day and much of the night they line up on Decatur Street, between Jackson Square and the Jackson Brewery, nonplussed in their floppy hats, big plastic sunglasses, flowers, and during Mardi Gras, seasonal plastic beads. In the old days, horses pulled the buggies; after a couple of mid-summer collapses, they were replaced by the more heat-tolerant mules. Depending on the weather, the mules hang around till midnight, picking up tourists for a half-hour spin around the Quarter. The buggy companies, including **Mid-City Carriages** (tel 504/581–4415), **Good Old Days Buggies** (tel 504/523–0804), and **Gay 90s Carriage Tours** (tel 504/943–8820), all offer about the same deals. Private buggies are $40 for a half-hour tour; they accommodate up to four riders, and they'll drop you off at any Quarter hotel when you're done. The larger surreys (with the fringe on top) are $8 a head, and the drivers wait around till they get six riders.

Either way you go, this is one of those tourists-only type of events—no romance-minded local couple ever saunters down to the Quarter to snuggle up on a buggy ride with a bottle of champagne. But if you're in the mood to *clop-clop*, here's a tip: the quality of the ride will depend mainly on your driver. On a private tour, you can request either a narrated or quiet trip; the group surreys are all narrated. Some of the city's most colorful characters have paid their dues as buggy operators: it would be worth going back in time to take a spin with bluesman J. Monque'D at the reins. One prominent local attorney put himself through law school on a buggy; he billed himself as the "Ben Hur of Bourbon Street." If you have the time, it's worth it to hang out for a couple minutes and talk to the drivers, to get a sense of who will tell the stories with élan, and who'll just repeat the local history and lore in a disinterested monotone.

Of course, don't write any dissertations based on the "history and highlights" you'll hear during those 30 minutes. Buggy drivers are notorious for mixing fact and fable: when you hear about the House of the Rising Sun or the haunted mansion, just enjoy it for the story it is. And when a buggy driver points out a restaurant and says that it's the best food in town, especially the crawfish platter, which has the best price, et cetera, et cetera... well, just enjoy it for the hustle it is.

See-and-be-scenes... If New Orleans has a Greenwich Village, it is the lively **intersection of Frenchmen and Chartres streets in the Faubourg Marigny.** In the span of a few blocks are some of the town's hippest clubs: **Cafe Brasil, Siam Cafe, Rubyfruit Jungle, Snug Harbor,** and **Check Point Charlie's** (see The Club Scene). Lining the sidewalk are tables occupied by skinny guys in goatees and young women with back tattoos, while gutter punks with nose rings and pierced tongues wander the block, bumming for change or selling videotapes. Often, the curb crowd outnumbers the paid customers inside the clubs, and for good reason: with the music usually spilling through the doors onto the street, you can hear plenty without paying a nickel. The sounds that flood this area are eclectic, ranging from Latin to klezmer to jazz. The sole requirement is a groove: this may be the only town where hipsters drop their attitude to do the mambo. The corner rocks the hardest during festival season; it's not unusual to see a drumming corps or a brass band take over the street, traffic be damned.

Another favorite streetside scene is at the **Maple Leaf Club.** Nothing but a single glass door separates Oak Street from the stage of this Uptown nightclub, and that door is often left open during the summer months. The result: a sidewalk of dancers, especially for Cajun and zydeco shows. For college students, check out the Maple Street strip near **Bruno's** and **TJ Quills,** or the corner near **The Boot** (see The Bar Scene).

Coffee shops... It's the cheapest rent in town: for about 85¢, a cup of coffee will hold you a table for the night. Few places will exert any subtle pressure to move you along,

with the occasional exception of **Cafe du Monde** (tel 504/
525–4544; 800 Decatur St., French Quarter), that large,
indoor/outdoor landmark across Decatur Street from
Jackson Square. This is the one place every visitor discovers, though locals do come here, too. Open 24 hours, it can
really bustle during peak hours, but it usually provides a
good opportunity to rest your feet or write postcards—
which will probably get dusted with the powdered sugar
that blows off the beignets (puffy, deep-fried square
doughnuts). Whether or not you like Cafe du Monde's
coffee depends on how you feel about two things: chicory
and steamed milk. Ground chicory root is what gives the
traditional café au lait its distinctive flavor. If you don't like
it, move along: this is the only type of coffee available here.

Some proud locals will say that this city likes its coffee strong, but they haven't yet registered the fact that the
rest of the country is drinking their coffee stronger.
Actually, full-scale coffee culture hasn't really caught on in
New Orleans. For example, there is no Starbucks backlash here—because there's no Starbucks. Few places serve
really great brew, and they all seem to be getting their
pastries from the same lousy bakery. The best cup of joe
in town is at the **Daily Planet Espresso Bar** (tel 504/
866–0651; 1039 Broadway, Uptown), but the only seating
is a few tables on the sidewalk. There's more activity at
Kaldi's Coffeehouse (tel 504/586–8989; 941 Decatur
St., French Quarter): at any given time, the clientele in
this spacious hall may include Quarter punks, tarot card
readers, lost tourists, and local professionals scanning
today's *Wall Street Journal*. The coffee ice-cream drinks
here are especially good; the pastries aren't. **Rue deLa
Course II** (tel 504/899–0242; 3128 Magazine St.,
Uptown) is the king of the Uptown coffeehouses.
Laptop-toting grad students compete for tables with
game players (Scrabble, backgammon, and chess are
available at the counter for the unprepared). On Sunday,
Rue Two is packed with readers of the *New York Times,*
which is available for purchase. With jazz music and picture windows overlooking Magazine Street, Rue Two's
ambiance is much better than its only-average coffee—
not to mention those same crummy pastries. Finally, the
cooperatively run **Neutral Ground** (tel 504/891–3381;
5110 Danneel St., Uptown) brings back the sixties spirit,
with live folk music nightly, and lots of gentle people.

NEW ORLEANS ⟨ **HANGING OUT**

A grave matter... Nope. Don't even think about it. Tantalizingly close to the French Quarter are the historic **St. Louis Cemeteries Nos. 1 and 2** (tel 504/482-5065), located on Basin Street and Claiborne Avenue, respectively. Above-ground, houselike tombs give the graveyards of New Orleans their macabre nickname, "Cities of the Dead." (Indeed, Mark Twain once said that New Orleans had no architecture except in its cemeteries.) In modern days, these landmarks have become famous as sets for movies, from *Easy Rider* to *Interview with the Vampire.* While they may seem quaint and spooky now, this mode of "burial" was a necessary way of life in the early days, since the ground hereabouts is actually below sea level; as one mid-19th-century journalist wrote in *DeBow's Review,* "I have watched the bailing out of the grave, the floating of the coffin, and have heard the friends of the deceased deplore this mode of interment." Among the occupants of St. Louis 1 and 2 are pirates (Dominique You, captain under Jean Lafitte) and poets (jazzman and author Danny Barker), though the most famous resident is the legendary priestess of voodoo, Marie Laveau—hers is the tomb that all the adventurous folks visit, to leave gifts and inscribe an "X." But don't you dare consider venturing into these graveyards after dark. The cemeteries all close their gates by late afternoon, and no visitors or tours may enter. A few foolhardy souls have jumped the fences to leave their mark on Laveau's tomb, but earthly threats far outnumber the spectral ones: day and night, the cemeteries are the surest places in the city to get robbed.

Safest walks... New Orleans is one of those cities in which everyone from your cabbie to your concierge will tell you not go out walking at night. Unfortunately, they're right. The Moon Walk, the Mississippi River levee, the parks, and all the other nice paths and lanes should be avoided after sundown. In general, it's only safe to stroll the fairly crowded, well-lit streets of the **French Quarter,** and then not alone. It's okay to walk around the new entertainment district along **Decatur Street** from the **House of Blues** (tel 504/529-1421; 225 Decatur St.) to **Planet Hollywood** (tel 504/522-7826; 620 Decatur St.) and the **Hard Rock Cafe** (tel 504/529-5617; 219 N. Peters St.), during the hours that these places are open.

The walk up Decatur Street takes you past plenty of late-night music clubs, bars, and restaurants, including **Jimmy Buffet's Margaritaville Cafe** (tel 504/592–2565; 1104 Decatur St.), **Coop's** (tel 504/525–9053; 1109 Decatur St.), and **Molly's at the Market** (tel 504/561–9473; 1107 Decatur St.). You can cut over to the **French Market** (tel 504/522–2621, 1008 N. Peters St.), where there's something open all around the clock, or continue up Decatur to Esplanade Avenue, and cross to the night-owl haven of the **Faubourg Marigny** (see "See-and-be-scenes", above). Even Jackson Square gets a little eerie at night as folks bed down on the benches, but **Pat O'Brien's** (tel 504/525–4823; 718 St. Peter St.) keeps St. Peter Street pretty busy. Probably the safest place in town is the commercial section of **Bourbon Street**; here, the most serious threats to your pocketbook are your own.

In search of vampires and other suckers... In the wake of *Interview with the Vampire*, there's been a red tide of late-night French Quarter ghost and vampire tours. Of course, the stories they tell may not have been authenticated by a team of independent scholars—but who cares? With the philosophy that the only thing you really have to fear is a dull tour, **Magic Walking Tours** (tel 504/593–9693) piles on the drama for its "Vampire and Ghost Hunt." This three-hour expedition meets at 8pm nightly at the candlelit **Lafitte's Blacksmith Shop** (tel 504/523–0066; 941 Bourbon St., French Quarter), and moves furtively through dimly lit residential sections of the lower Quarter. In the light of day, the tales of fire-perished people whose screams still resound through the old square may be a little hard to swallow. But on a night tour, with the right amount of solemnity, it can be as convincing as a good campfire story. It's also the safest way to explore the Quarter at night.

Marketing savvy... In its halcyon days, the **Farmer's Market** (tel 504/522–2621; 1235 N. Peters St., French Quarter) must have been a wonderful and boisterous place. Farmers would arrive in the dark of night, and sleep in their wagons until the shoppers and restaurateurs arrived to pick through the produce. Vendors sold fresh fruits, vegetables, fish, and meats; one can only imagine the sights and sounds, not to mention the smells. This market kept bustling for decades: it wasn't too long ago that the chefs of the best French Quarter restaurants would arrive at daybreak to purchase fresh ingredients for the day's feasts. These days signs hang all around the empty stalls, promising a revival of the old market. It hasn't happened yet: only a couple of fruit and vegetable stands remain. One of these is open 24 hours, and it's run by an old-timer who will take the time to explain his regional produce, which includes Creole tomatoes, Vidalia sweet onions, lurid red Louisiana strawberries, fat mirlitons (a local squashlike vegetable), and satsumas (a sweet citrus fruit that has to be tasted to be believed). There's also a 24-hour specialty grocer that sells tourist-oriented products, such as cookbooks and hot sauces (the price is higher than local supermarkets, but ambiance ain't cheap). The traffic picks up on weekends, when a flea market takes over, with vendors peddling such valuables as tube socks, cheap sunglasses, weird military memorabilia, T-shirts with outdated slogans like "Where's the Beef" and "Me So Horny," and even a few stalls of nothing but good, solid junk.

Shopping on Bourbon Street... It doesn't take long to discover that the stores here are much less than they seem (and they never seemed that much to begin with). If the sign says "art gallery," it's a poster shop. If it's a "factory outlet," it's stocked with the same T-shirts, magnets, and little white ceramic Mardi Gras masks that all the other shops are selling. Look closely at that "Special Sale" sign: it may be permanently attached to the wall. And most of all, beware the adult bookstores with the video rooms in the back: the first thing you see when you walk into the viewing booth may be a hole in the wall, with a little eyeball staring curiously at you. For adult magazines, go to the enigmatically named **All That Jazz** (tel 504/522–5657; 419 Bourbon St.). **Lust is Life Condom Co.** (tel 504/529–4942; 323 Bourbon St.) has varying types, sizes, and colors of its eponymous prophylactic, though not as much as you'd expect in a shop that's named for them.

A few blocks down Bourbon is the **Marie Laveau House of Voodoo** (tel 504/581–3751; 739 Bourbon St.), which bills itself as a museum. If so, it has quite a small museum-to-gift-shop ratio. Three little storefront-style tableaux of Africa, Haiti, and New Orleans fill the back wall; the rest of these two rooms contain shelves lined with books, incense, candles, voodoo dolls, dried alligator heads, and a fairly interesting and decently priced collection of South and Central American and Mexican masks. As you might expect from its Bourbon Street location, this shop camps it up a little: the "no pictures" signs warn that you may lose your cameras or "your soul."

Walking into the **Hungry Artists Studio** (tel 504/523–6857; 632 Bourbon St.) is a bit surreal. Located in the thick of the strip, this quiet studio shop is run by a nice, mannered couple from Minnesota who sell cards and prints with line illustrations of French Quarter landmarks. They seem almost oblivious to their location; it's like Lake Wobegon on Bourbon Street.

Other late shopping... Canal Street rolls up its sidewalks by 6pm, and the Riverwalk mall closes its doors at 9pm (10pm on weekends). After that, there's not much opportunity for shopping, unless you're looking for books or music. Late hours are kept by a number of local record stores; the biggie is **Tower Records** (tel 504/529–4411; 408 N. Peters St.), which is open nightly until midnight. This French Quarter outlet of the international chain has a listening center, a Ticketmaster desk, a surprisingly good selection of relevant books and magazines, and lots of CDs and tapes. Local music is on the second floor. Next door is **Tower Video** (tel 504/581–2012; 410 N. Peters St.), which has videos from local artists for sale, as well as a good selection of general, foreign, and cult movies for rent. One of the city's best-stocked bookstores is also open late: **Bookstar** (tel 504/523–6411; 414 N. Peters St.), which is right near Tower Records (many people assume this two-story shop is part of the Tower record/video complex). While there are no tables or comfy easy chairs here, late-night shoppers usually plunk down in the aisles to browse through their purchases. The regional shelves are well-stocked, and there's a good magazine rack.

If your idea of a record store is a dusty room packed with boxes of vinyl, check out **Rock N Roll Records and Collectibles** (tel 504/561–5683; 1214 Decatur St.), also in the French Quarter. On the same block is **Jazzology/Audiofile Records** (tel 504/525–1776; 1206 Decatur St.), which is really another name for the record stand in the

NEW ORLEANS (HANGING OUT)

Palm Court Jazz Cafe. Come here for traditional jazz vinyl and CDs.

Just off Canal Street in the French Quarter, **Unique General Store** (tel 504/586–0102; 127 Royal St.), an old-style newsstand that's open until midnight, comes complete with a cigar counter, racing forms, international newspapers, adult stuff in the back, and a grizzled old man at the cash register. Uptown, college students go late to **Mushroom Records** (tel 504/866–6065; 1037 Broadway), which shares a corner with the Boot bar and the Daily Planet Espresso Bar. In addition to new and used CDs, the Mushroom sells smoking material and kitschy dorm room decor.

The biggest inventory of adult books and movies is near the airport, at the 24-hour **Airline Adult Books** (tel 504/468–2931; 1406 26th St., Kenner). This large store has thousands of videos, books, magazines, and sex novelties. Private screening rooms are available for the enigmatic price of $5.44, plus a $10 key deposit.

Best moonlit view of the city... By far, the best way to look at this town is from a 33rd-floor seat on the revolving carousel lounge of the **Top of the Mart** (tel 504/522–9795), downtown at the International Trade Mart (see The Bar Scene). Though not as encompassing, the view from the **Canal Street Ferry** (tel 504/364–8114. foot of Canal Street) is lovely in early evening. This is a strictly utilitarian boat: the ferry is one means of connecting the East and West banks of the Mississippi. It's a short ride, but fun—you may even find yourself in a quick game of pitching quarters with the ferry operators. The trip is free for pedestrians; cars pay a toll only on the return trip.

When it's sailing, the 24-hour **Flamingo Casino** (tel 800/587–5825 or 504/587–7777; 610 S. Peters St., Downtown) would seem to be a good way to cruise the Mississippi and see Downtown and the French Quarter. But since sight-seeing riders aren't gambling riders, there are no seats provided on the outside deck. Plus, the electronic *cheeping* of slot machines isn't really the most appropriate soundtrack for gazing at the city (although local cynics might disagree).

Mass appeal... And now for something completely different: you could go to church. **The St. Louis Cathedral**

(tel 504/525–9585; Jackson Sq., French Quarter) is the building that best defines New Orleans spiritual life, with the possible exception of Jimmy Swaggart's old Airline Highway motel room. The first church on this site, an adobe-and-wood structure, was destroyed by a 1723 hurricane; the second was lost in the Good Friday fire of 1788. The Spanish-style structure that now stands was built in 1794 for about $50,000. It isn't the Quarter's oldest building—the Ursuline Convent and Lafitte's Blacksmith Shop, among others, preceded it. Still, the Cathedral looms with authority over the Quarter, safe in the knowledge that nobody will ever turn this one into a casino or theme restaurant. Among the highlights of St. Louis' recent history was a 1987 visit by Pope John Paul II; this trip marked one of the first times that souvenir hawkers went full-tilt into developing a papal line of products, including the infamous Pope Soap on a Rope. Tours of the Cathedral's gilded interior are only offered during the day, but a 6pm Saturday mass is open to visitors. If you're in town during a religious holiday, call to find out if late Masses are being offered. This is a regal place to be for Midnight Mass on Christmas Eve.

late nigh

7

t dining

The bright lights of
Crescent City dining dim
early. By 11pm, the
illustrious single-name
joints—Antoine's,
Arnaud's, Brennan's,
Galatoire's, et cetera—

have served up their last saucy meal. A new scene begins; the Clover Grill blooms and the Hummingbird takes wing. The gourmets retire for the evening, to be replaced by hordes of hungry post-bar crowds combing the town for a late-night Southern breakfast, a fried seafood po-boy basket, or a really fat cheeseburger. New Orleanians, like vampires, develop new tastes at night.

Night diners don't necessarily have their minds just on food, either. You can eat gumbo while you bowl at Mid-City. Snap your fingers to jazz while you click your chopsticks at Funky Butt. Or take a ringside seat for a little free people-watching at Cafe Du Monde, the Mardi Gras Truck Stop, or Lucky Cheng's. And even with many of the top-name joints closed, you can find local food favorites, such as jambalaya, red beans, oysters, and bread pudding, all ready to stay up with you.

French Quarter Late Night Dining

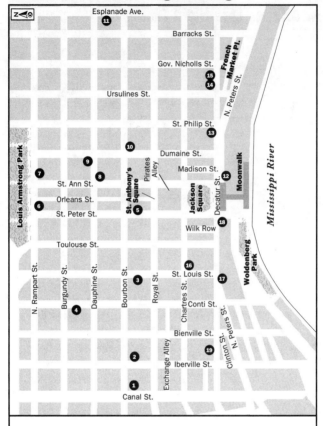

The Bombay Club **4**

Cafe du Monde **12**

Clover Grill **10**

Coop's Place **15**

Donna's Bar & Grill **7**

Felix's Restaurant and
   Oyster Bar **2**

Funky Butt **6**

Hard Rock Cafe **17**

House of Blues **19**

Kaldi's Coffeehouse **13**

Krystal's **1**

Lucky Cheng's **3**

Molly's at the Market **14**

Napoleon House **16**

Planet Hollywood **18**

Poppy's Grill **5**

Port of Call **11**

Quarter Scene **9**

St. Ann's Deli **8**

148

New Orleans Late Night Dining

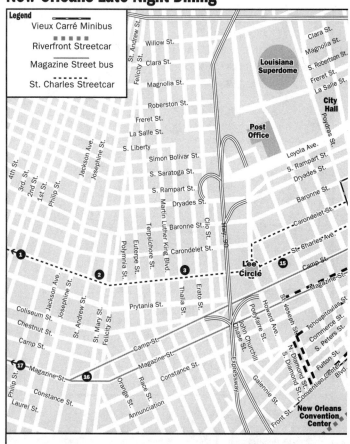

Bailey's **5**
Cafe Roma **16, 6**
Camellia Grill **1**
Check Point Charlie's **10**
Cooter Brown's **1**

Hummingbird Hotel & Grill **15**
Le Bon Temps Roule **17**
Mardi Gras Truck Stop **13**
Mid-City Lanes **4**
New Showcase Lounge **7**

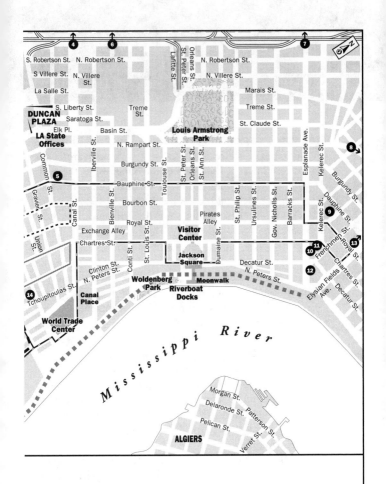

La Peniche **9**

Praline Connection **11**

Rick's Famous Pancake Cottage **1**

Rivershack Tavern **1**

Rocky & Carlo's **8**

St. Charles Tavern **3**

Siam Cafe **12**

The Trolley Stop **2**

Vic's Kangaroo Cafe **14**

After the show... Located across the street from the Orpheum Theatre and just a few blocks from the Saenger Theatre, **Bailey's** sees the hungriest of the post-symphony and theater crowd. Once Downtown's only all-night restaurant (except for the Hummingbird, which is a different animal entirely), this attractive Fairmont Hotel cafe now closes at midnight on weekends. Basics are good here, such as soups and sandwiches; the smoked chicken and corn bisque is nice and thick, and the pastas are recommended. Come here if you're out late, and you don't want to go slumming. In the nearby upper Quarter, the stately **Bombay Club** has scaled back its night menu; at 11pm this British-style bar starts serving only burgers, omelettes, and waffles. Also in the Quarter, the historic **Napoleon House** is a popular place to retire post-show. A bust of the Emperor himself wildly looks down from the cash register, and the speakers pipe out continuous classical music. The menu includes warm muffulettas (a popular local sandwich of meats, cheeses, and olive salad on a round loaf of Italian bread), soups, salads, and nice cheese trays.

Both performers and audience members frequent two casual but charming restaurants, the **Quarter Scene** and the Faubourg Marigny's **La Peniche**. Both offer extensive menus with a regional emphasis; specials might include Creole meatloaf or shrimp appetizers. Of course, if the show you saw was a movie, a visit to **Planet Hollywood** in the French Quarter would continue the night's theme. The menu includes the large Hollywood Bowl salad and creative regional offerings like crawfish lasagna and barbecue shrimp pizza. And if you spent the night at a rock or rap show at the State Palace, just follow the crowd across Canal Street to the French Quarter's

Krystal's, a brightly lit three-story shrine to little, flat, square, perfectly tasteless hamburgers, affectionately referred to by some people as "sliders."

Best bar food... When the shortest possible distance between a bar and a restaurant is a wobbly line, it helps if the bar you're in has its own kitchen in the back. Chances are good that it will—indeed, the city's best taverns turn out some surprisingly good meals. It's all part of a deeply felt ethic here: everything is better with a plate of food in front of it. One of the trustiest kitchens belongs to the **Rivershack Tavern**, out in suburban Jefferson, which also attracts a sizable lunch and dinner crowd. The New Orleans and Southern fare here include shrimp remoulade, fried green tomatoes, and great fried chicken. The "Causeway Special" sandwich—possibly the only meal in town named after a bridge—is half shrimp and half oyster. In the Garden District, **Le Bon Temps Roule** has superior versions of bar food standbys, such as buffalo wings, nachos, and quesadillas; Yankee food such as grinders, Philly cheese steaks, and New York–style pretzels assuage the cravings of the East Coast–bred Tulane students who fill this place on weekends. Another bar popular with the college crowd is Uptown at **Cooter Brown's**, which layers its sandwiches with pastrami that's imported from Chicago. Both Bon Temps and Cooter's also please local palates with Louisiana delicacies, such as crawfish boudin (intestinal casing stuffed with spicy rice, pork, and crawfish that tastes better than it sounds) and alligator sausage.

Where to have breakfast anytime... If you're hungering for the sizzle of sausage patties and the crackle of frying eggs, there are several 24-hour joints to check out. The **Hummingbird Hotel & Grill** is the quintessential downtown breakfast dive. It's open all night, the juke box is one of the best in town, and there's even a hotel on the second floor (not recommended unless you're trying to write the next great American beat novel). For greasy breakfast food, the Hummingbird can't be beat: flaky biscuits, creamy grits, good bacon and sausage (stay away from the pork chops), all probably served by some tattooed guy named Sal. In case you haven't guessed, the neighborhood is a little shaky.

Located on Bourbon Street near several gay bars, **The Clover Grill** has as its motto, "Simple food for a complex community." Offerings include very good "Geaux Girl Waffles," and even a bowl of Fruit Loops for $1.59 (a banana is an extra 69¢). The juke box plays plenty of disco, and the lively scene attracts gays and adventurous straights. The menu itself is full of bathroom-stall humor—copies are frequently stolen from the restaurant as souvenirs of local culture. That they are. Clover's "sister restaurant" up Bourbon Street, **Poppy's Grill**, is right across the street from Pat O'Brien's, which results in a steady stream of Hurricane-blown tourists. Breakfast specials start at 5am.

If you're looking for something a bit more decorous, **The Trolley Stop** on St. Charles Avenue in the Garden District is a new 24-hour restaurant with wooden floors, lots of streetcar prints on the walls, and even a *faux* streetcar facade. The Trolley's menu literally has pages of breakfast items, including liver and eggs; biscuits and gravy (not always easy to find in this town); oatmeal; and all kinds of pancakes, waffles, and omelettes. Once known for its bygone collection of vintage lunchboxes, **Rick's Famous Pancake Cottage** is a local favorite for 'cakes. The Uptown branch is open through the weekend with an International House of Pancakes–style selection of fruit toppings and syrups.

The biggest and best burgers... It's a gastronomic fact: the later the hour, the greater the appetite for real big burgers. Each kitchen claims that its burgers are the biggest and best. Actually, most of the burgers weigh in at about a half-pound, and the accessories are fairly identical. One of the standouts is in the French Quarter at **Port of Call**, which is recommended for one delicious topping: the savory, red wine–soaked, sautéed mushrooms. Also in the Quarter, **Molly's at the Market** gets a nod for widest gourmet selection: the stuffed burger fillings include feta, spinach, and blue cheese. The **Clover Grill** is most famous for its preparation: the burgers are grilled beneath an actual automobile hubcap, a tradition here since this diner first opened on Bourbon Street in the 1950s. You can also watch the preparation at Uptown's classy **Camellia Grill**; when the cook squirts cooking oil on the meat, you can just hear your arteries slam shut. It's only well-bred beef at **The Bombay Club**, which is decorated like an English gentlemen's establishment. The burgers in this upper Quarter bar/restaurant are also dressed up in British fashion, with a thick wedge of ripe Stilton cheese. Of course, if what you truly want is really little hamburgers, you can always hit **Krystal's** on Bourbon Street for its tiny sandwiches, small enough to be consumed by the six-pack.

Sound bites... You never need to choose between food and music in New Orleans; most music clubs have kitchens that stay open till the final encore or the last waltz. Greasy food meets grungy tunes at **Check Point Charlie's** in the Faubourg Marigny, where fried burgers, chicken, and fish make a perfect accompaniment for high-decibel rock. Australian food meets American blues when **Vic's Kangaroo Cafe**, in the Warehouse District, offers a small but charming selection of meat pies and rolls from Down Under. **Mid-City Lanes,** that delightful bowling alley/music club in Mid-City, has both classic New Orleans music and munchies; the latter includes great po-boys, gumbo, and bread pudding. On weekends, the **Rivershack Tavern** out in Jefferson has a raucous college and yuppie dance crowd that comes in for blues and rockabilly, and fuels up from one of the city's best late-night menus. For the bohemian experience, take a seat on a floor pillow at **Siam Cafe** (also called the Dragon's Den), which serves Thai food in the Faubourg Marigny to the varied tunes of local up-and-coming bands. Down the street in the French Quarter, **Kaldi's** usually enhances the boho coffeehouse atmosphere with a weekend jazz trio.

Soul food and soulful jazz... The city's newest jazz clubs all serve food that fits the down-home, neighborhood ambiance. Try the barbecue beef tips and jambalaya at **Donna's Bar & Grill** in the French Quarter, which also has jars of pickled pigs' lips at the bar. Out in Gentilly, **The New Showcase Lounge** offers trays of delicious smothered pork chops, turkey wings, and stewed chicken; the food is usually depleted by midnight or so. On the northern edge of the French Quarter, **Funky Butt** offers a wonderful cultural hybrid of jazz

NEW ORLEANS (LATE NIGHT DINING

plus Vietnamese food, such as barbecue black molasses baby back ribs, served with ginger yam and snow peas; if you want to go soul, you can also find okra gumbo and great bread pudding here.

Turning the volume down... If loud live music or juke boxes is the last thing you want to hear, try the **Napoleon House,** which plays nonstop classical music that's as soothing as the historic French Quarter restaurant's bowls of thick, hearty soup. **The Quarter Scene** (in the French Quarter, naturally) and **La Peniche** in the Faubourg Marigny are both subdued little cafes filled with plants and the hum of quiet conversation. But if you really want to get away from it all, try your luck at **The Bombay Club**, also in the Quarter, which has a few tables equipped with curtains. Just pull 'em shut and tune 'em out.

One more cup of coffee... As you sit down at a table at **Cafe du Monde**, rest assured that you have left the modern era of dizzying coffee choices. Nowhere in this French Quarter landmark is there a large chalkboard listing espressos, lattes, or flavor syrups. It's all the same drink here: café au lait, a milky combo of dark roast coffee and chicory, served in a cup and saucer. That's it, except for the new iced café au lait, hot chocolate (very frothy and good), milk, or orange juice. Be prepared when your brisk server speeds by to take your order. Payment is expected upon delivery. If a double decaf cap is more your speed, saunter a couple blocks down the street to **Kaldi's Coffeehouse**, a comfortable, always busy Quarter coffeehouse located in a former bank. This is the place for frozen coffee drinks, which are big sellers in the summer months—about half the year in this town.

The chain gang... Hard Rock Cafe, House of Blues, and **Planet Hollywood** have been pilloried enough in these pages, so they're granted this much: they all have late kitchens (the latest are Planet Hollywood and House of Blues). Sure, the local outlets of these chains are pretty much what you'll find in Los Angeles, London, or wherever. But when you're hungry and it's late, sometimes the last thing you want is a surprise. The Rock's big salads, big sandwiches, and big desserts are dependable. The

House has a great touch with Southern food like barbecue and mashed potatoes. And the Planet reserves much of its menu for New Orleans selections, including jambalaya, étouffée, and shrimp Creole. And though more expensive than most other places in town, their prices usually fall only couple of dollars of what you'd expect to pay elsewhere in the city. The only chain in this strip that closes early is the nearby **Fashion Cafe**, which shuts off its lights by 11pm—one can only suppose that supermodels need their sleep.

Veggies for vegetarians... In the old days, a salad in New Orleans was the shredded lettuce that's in a po-boy. Either that, or a pressed-wood, plastic-wrapped bowl that's been sitting in a refrigerator all day, which contains the exact same shredded lettuce as in that po-boy. But, for late-night dining, vegetarians now fare at least as well as their carnivorous companions. Maybe better. **Cafe Roma** is a handsome, upscale pizza place serving large spinach, Italian, and Caesar salads, as well as several vegetarian pies—pesto, spinach, artichoke, or eggplant. It has two locations, one in the Garden district and one in Mid-City. In the French Quarter, **Funky Butt** has a "funky vegetable lineup" of baby corn, snow peas, squash, straw mushrooms, cabbage, and carrots, served in Vietnamese meals with rice pancakes, noodles, or tofu. The best bet is curried merliton (a local squash) and whipped tofu, served over crunchy vegetables. On the other side of the Quarter is **Siam Cafe**, a laid-back Thai restaurant in the Faubourg Marigny. The upstairs kitchen stays open late, and seating is available at tables on the balcony, or inside on floor pillows. Siam offers numerous vegetarian dishes; be sure to start it all off with the delicate spring rolls. Finally, no vegetarian will find **Lucky Cheng's** menu to be a drag. This Asian-Creole restaurant in the French Quarter, famous for its Asian-American transvestite wait staff, will remove the meat from any of its stir-fry dishes. It also has a few vegetarian meals in its nightly specials; one of the best is a salad of roasted mushrooms and roasted eggplant.

Sugar, baby... You know that you've come to the right place when your counter waiter at Uptown's **Camellia Grill** asks if you'd like your chocolate pecan pie heated.

Then you watch as the cook slides it onto a smooth, sizzling griddle—no microwaves here. The chocolate melts into little lodes of goo inside the caramelized praline mixture, for one of the best taste experiences in town. Beignets—deep-fried, square doughnuts—are the only food served at **Cafe du Monde** in the French Quarter. Go around back to watch the beignets prepared in efficient, assembly-line fashion. They arrive barely visible under a mound of powdered sugar; don't sneeze, especially if your date is wearing black. Finally, Orleanians have very strong opinions about just who has the finest bread pudding, and there are an astonishing number of local variations on what sounds like a simple dessert. The rich praline topping at the **Praline Connection** bumps this Faubourg Marigny soul food restaurant's version to the top of the list. You can also find a great late-night candy counter here, filled with different flavors of some of the town's best pralines.

Out of the frying pan... As darkness falls, nobody cares if you're foregoing the salad with low-fat dressing for the plate of onion rings. This is especially true in the Big Greasy, a town that loves to fry (and it shows). Jefferson's **Rivershack Tavern** has a Louisiana veggie platter that includes fried green tomatoes, fried eggplant, fried pickles, fried sweet potatoes, and fried mushrooms. Uptown's **Cooter Brown's** adds cheesy "Cooter balls" to the mix, along with the much-loved fried soft-shell crab: a whole crab, claws and all, that comes out of the fryer looking every bit like a golden, crusty space monster. On Upper Bourbon Street, **Felix's Restaurant and Oyster Bar** makes delicate fried oysters that nearly explode in your mouth, while the Chalmette diner **Rocky & Carlo's** has fried shrimp, oysters, and catfish to boggle the mind. Uptown at the **Camellia Grill**, a man in a tuxedo will serve you chili cheese fries; eat them with pinky extended. And that great trucker favorite, the chicken fried steak, comes on a platter with fries at the **Clover Grill** on Bourbon Street, or is served in more fashionable Marigny surroundings at **La Peniche**.

New Orleans classics... Louis Armstrong used to sign his letters "Red Beans and Ricely Yours...," which gives some idea of the local affection for this combo.

Traditionally, this was Monday night dinner; the beans were left to simmer all day, allowing them to break and thicken while the Monday wash was coming clean. The secret to finding a good plate: make sure the kitchen allows plenty of time for the preparation. (You can't hurry love or red beans.) Some of the town's finest red beans and rice are in Faubourg Marigny at the **Praline Connection**, which also has white beans, crowder peas and okra, or other bean varieties.

Jambalaya is another beloved rice dish that varies even more widely in quality. Similar to rice dishes found throughout Mexico and South America, jambalaya often has a tomato flavor; ingredients may include chicken, turkey, seafood, andouille, ham, or green onions. Rabbit and sausage jambalaya is one specialty of **Coop's Place** in the French Quarter.

Oysters in the half shell are another local favorite, with oyster bars located right alongside drink bars at many taverns. Full-time shuckers split the salty bivalves and serve them by the half-dozen or dozen; it's your job to prepare your own dip from the available jars and bottles of condiments such as horseradish, Tabasco, and catsup. It's good to be careful about where you eat your oysters: **Felix's** in the French Quarter and **Cooter Brown's** Uptown are both fine choices. If it's your first time, you may want to slide that oyster onto a saltine; it takes a little conditioning to get used to the slimy texture.

Gumbo is more than a local dish; it has become a metaphor for the city. People here love to say that New Orleans is a big gumbo, both being filled with diverse and distinct ingredients that combine for a perfect flavor. It's our version of the melting pot. Gumbo usually comes in two varieties: seafood or chicken/turkey and sausage. Both are served with rice. Downtown at the Fairmont Hotel, **Bailey's** has a fine seafood gumbo; when that's closed, the **St. Charles Tavern** in the Garden District is the place for a 24-hour bowl. Speaking of bowl, the kitchen at Mid-City Lanes makes a delicious turkey and andouille gumbo.

Finally, a discussion of the classic cuisine of New Orleans would be incomplete without a mention of the ubiquitous **Lucky Dog**, available from weenie-shaped carts on corners throughout the French Quarter. These chili dogs were made infamous by John Kennedy Toole in his Pulitzer Prize–winning farce *A Confederacy of Dunces*. Read the book; skip the hot dog (no matter how lucky you're feeling).

Po-boys are our heros... Other cities may have their hero and sub sandwiches, but New Orleans is a town of po-boys. The po-boy comes in two sizes: whole loaf and half loaf. A half loaf is usually large enough for one person; it is, in fact, commonly divided in two sections. On crusty French bread sit a variety of fillings, including fried seafood, roast beef, hot or smoked sausage, and even potato. (Note: for some reason, hamburger po-boys are almost always bad choices.) The next decision is whether or not to have your po-boy "dressed," which means adorned with shredded lettuce, thinly sliced tomato, and pickles. Condiments include a local favorite: spicy Creole mustard. Finally, if your po-boy is to go, it's wrapped in white paper and held together by a piece of masking tape. And if your sandwich deviates in any way from the above description, you may as well hand it back right away: it ain't a po-boy. You're always in for the real deal at **Rocky & Carlo's** out in Chalmette, the **Mardi Gras Truck Stop** out in Gentilly, and, in the French Quarter, **St. Ann's Deli**.

Best for people-watching... One night about 4am, a man stumbled into the **Hummingbird Hotel & Grill**, wearing jeans, a T-shirt, and a cardboard Burger King crown. He announced in a loud voice that he was the King of Mardi Gras, and then pitched forward and landed on the floor. Welcome to the Hummingbird, a 24-hour joint downtown on St. Charles in the middle of New Orleans' version of the Bowery. For the price of a cup of coffee, you can take a side booth and watch a dazzling array of folks from all walks of life, staggering in at night's end for plate meals and breakfasts. A favorite of the most theatrical of the French Quarter gay population, the **Clover Grill** rivals the Bird in entertainment value. The cooks and waiters will, on occasion, abandon their posts to go to the window to loudly gossip about who's going into the bar across the street, and with whom. Meanwhile, the show is inside the restaurant at **Lucky Cheng's**, a French Quarter spot that employs only Asian-American transvestite servers. The **Mardi**

Gras Truck Stop is a different scene altogether. Tables are situated right in the middle of the store section of this active truck stop in Gentilly. After watching truckers come and go, buying gas and slurpees and belt buckles, you'll feel ready to climb in your rig and try to make Omaha by morning. Finally, as the name suggests, much of the world passes by **Cafe du Monde** at least once. This is one French Quarter place where locals go to watch tourists, who are a pretty entertaining bunch of people themselves.

The Index

$$$	$20–$30
$$	$12–$20
$	under $12

Prices are for a full meal, not including drinks and tip.

Bailey's. Open till midnight on weekends, this attractive Fairmont Hotel coffee shop is a favorite post-symphony and theater stop.... *Tel 504/529–7111. 123 Baronne St., Downtown. $$*

The Bombay Club. One of the Quarter's best late-night options: this courtly, English-themed bar serves burgers, omelettes, and waffles on weekend nights from 11pm to 2am.... *Tel 504/586–0972. 830 Conti St., French Quarter. $*

Cafe du Monde. The name isn't hyperbole: everyone in the world really does seem to stop by at least once to try the fried, sugar-drenched beignets and chicory-laced café au lait.... *Tel 504/525–4544. 800 Decatur St., French Quarter. No credit cards. $*

Cafe Roma. Open nightly till 1am, this local favorite has gourmet pizzas, pasta, hot sandwiches, and great salads, in a clean, attractive setting.... *Garden District: tel 504/524–2419, 1901 Sophie Wright Place; Mid-City: tel 504/827–2300, 3340 Bienville St. DC not accepted. $*

Camellia Grill. Open until 1am weeknights and 3am weekends, this is a one-of-a-kind New Orleans late-night eatery, and a favorite of politico James Carville. This counterspace-only joint has all the trappings of a gourmet restaurant, including a maitre d' and a tuxedoed server.... *Tel 504/866–9573. 626 S. Carrollton Ave., Uptown. No credit cards. $*

Check Point Charlie's. This good, greasy rock club has burgers, fish fillets, chicken nuggets, and other food, all good and greasy.... *Tel 504/949–7012. 501 Esplanade Ave., Faubourg Marigny. D, DC not accepted. $*

Clover Grill. A 24-hour place that's unique, even for New Orleans. The ambience combines a classic fifties diner with a nineties gay bar.... *Tel 504/523–0904. 900 Bourbon St., French Quarter. D, DC not accepted. $*

Coop's Place. Tourists and regulars come here for late drinks and regional food, such as jambalaya, gumbo, and blackened redfish.... *Tel 504/525–9053. 1109 Decatur St., French Quarter. $*

Cooter Brown's. This very popular bar brings in college students with iron stomachs who down spicy alligator sausage, crawfish boudin, and big bowls of chili, then polish it all off with a half-dozen raw oysters.... *Tel 504/866–9104. 509 S. Carrollton Ave., Uptown. DC not accepted. $*

Donna's Bar & Grill. This funky jazz and brass band club serves up down-home food as well as a fine musical menu.... *Tel 504/596–6914. 800 N. Rampart St., French Quarter. No credit cards. $*

Felix's Restaurant and Oyster Bar. Located right off upper Bourbon Street, this oyster bar has a polished look and an extensive menu of seafood sandwiches and plates. You can't go wrong with any of the oyster dishes. Open weeknights till midnight, weekends till 1am.... *Tel 504/522–4440. 739 Iberville St., French Quarter. D not accepted. $$*

Funky Butt. If you can get past the name (which comes from a legendary old jazz hall), this new music club is a great place for late-night Vietnamese food. In keeping with the theme, why not try the vermicelli with charbroiled pork butt, or perhaps "Richard's Big Ass Pig Ass Sandwich"?.... *Tel 504/558–0872. 714 N. Rampart St., French Quarter. AE, D, DC not accepted. $*

Hard Rock Cafe. Open till midnight on weekends, this familiar chain serves much of the same stuff you'll find in all the other Rocks, which isn't all that bad, especially the lime chicken and watermelon ribs.... *Tel 504/529–5617. 219 N. Peters St., French Quarter. D, DC not accepted. $*

House of Blues. This music club has a separate restaurant area, with plenty of wood-backed booths and tables. The Southern-style food is good, and the night's show plays on monitors.... *Tel 504/529–2583. 225 Decatur St., French Quarter. Reservations only for those going to the club, or for parties of 10. DC not accepted. $$*

Hummingbird Hotel & Grill. One of the best bowls of grits in town is served at this greasiest of greasy spoons, a destination for cab drivers, cops, and the post-bar crowd. A must-see for slummers.... *Tel 504/523–9165. 804 St. Charles Ave., Downtown. No credit cards. $*

Kaldi's Coffeehouse. An easy mix of tourists and local Quarter characters come to this laid-back coffeehouse for wondrous ice-cream coffee drinks and so-so pastries. The price of a cup of coffee will give you table privileges all night.... *Tel 504/586–8989. 940 Decatur St., French Quarter. No credit cards. $*

Krystal's. This 24-hour chain serves little square burgers similar to White Castle's. The location is ideal for a post–Bourbon Street junk food binge.... *Tel 504/523–4030. 116 Bourbon St., French Quarter. No credit cards. $*

Le Bon Temps Roule. Popular with college students and neighborhood regulars, this funky bar has a good late kitchen. Try the baked potato with a roast beef and gravy topping.... *Tel 504/895–8117. 4801 Magazine St., Garden District. DC not accepted. $*

Lucky Cheng's. Usually open till 11:30pm or midnight, this "Asian Creole" restaurant has good stir-fry and memorable transvestite servers.... *Tel 504/529–2045. 720 St. Louis St., French Quarter. $$$*

Lucky Dog. Sold from carts throughout the French Quarter, these literary links were popularized in John Kennedy Toole's *A Confederacy of Dunces*. They're a local tradition, sort of.... *Tel 504/523–9260. Various sites, French Quarter. $*

Mardi Gras Truck Stop. Not only truckers consider this a 24-hour po-boy palace. Tables are on two floors, as well as in a television room.... *Tel 504/945–1000. 2401 Elysian Fields Ave., Gentilly. DC not accepted. $*

Mid-City Lanes. The kitchen at this music club/bowling alley stays open as long as the music plays, and serves surprisingly skillful versions of New Orleans classics, such as onion mumms (fried onions), and andouille and turkey gumbo.... *Tel 504/482–3133. 4133 Carrollton Ave., Mid-City. D, DC not accepted. $ (About $5 cover during live music.)*

Molly's at the Market. This bar is a favorite of Quarter nightcrawlers, who show up here at the end of their rounds for half-pound burgers stuffed with such ingredients as feta, marinara, or blue cheese.... *Tel 504/561–9473. 1107 Decatur St., French Quarter. $*

Napoleon House. Napoleon never made it to his home-in-exile, but this European-style cafe is a favorite of locals and tourists. The warm muffuletta is a house specialty. Open weeknights till midnight and weekends till 1am.... *Tel 504/ 524–9752. 500 Chartres St., French Quarter. Reservations for parties of 8. $$$*

New Showcase Lounge. This neighborhood jazz club serves great soul food till it runs out, usually 'round midnight.... *Tel 504/945–5612. 1915 N. Broad St., Gentilly. $*

La Peniche. This friendly Marigny restaurant doesn't do anything great, but it does several things quite well, including crawfish étouffée, pork roast, and rotisserie chicken.... *Tel 504/ 943–1460. 1940 Dauphine St., Faubourg Marigny. D not accepted. $$$*

Planet Hollywood. Yes, it's a national chain, but corporate executive chef Beany Macgregor is a native son, which helps explain its confident spins on local classics, such as crawfish andouille pizza and Cajun eggrolls. Open till 1am.... *Tel 504/522–7826. 620 Decatur St., French Quarter. D not accepted. $$$*

Poppy's Grill. This 24-hour diner is located across the street from Pat O'Brien's; come here to ladle some grits and eggs

NEW ORLEANS ⏐ LATE NIGHT DINING

atop your Hurricanes.... *Tel 504/524–3287. 717 St. Peter St., French Quarter. D, DC not accepted. $*

Port of Call. Open till midnight on weeknights and 3am weekends, this is often the first place locals think of for late-night eats. The burgers are big, the steaks so-so; stay away from the pizza.... *Tel 504/523–0120. 838 Esplanade Ave., French Quarter. No credit cards. $*

Praline Connection. Open till midnight on weekends, this efficient soul food restaurant is located in a popular music club neighborhood, making it a good pre-club dinner stop. Leave room for dessert.... *Tel 504/943–3934. 542 Frenchmen St., Faubourg Marigny. $*

Quarter Scene. Open till midnight, this quaint, plant-filled cafe serves as a second kitchen for many of its Quarterite regulars.... *Tel 504/522–6533. 900 Dumaine St., French Quarter. Closed Tues. DC not accepted. $$$*

Rick's Famous Pancake Cottage. Just as the name suggests, this is the place for 'cakes, with plenty of gooey fruit topping and whipped cream, if desired. Note: Rick's has a Canal Street location that's only open for breakfast and lunch.... *Tel 504/822–2630. 1438 S. Carrollton Ave., Uptown. $*

Rivershack Tavern. This attractive, old-style saloon serves everything from fried pickles to alligator pizza.... *Tel 504/ 837–7118. 3449 River Rd., Jefferson. $*

Rocky & Carlo's. Whether you're talking hair or food, folks in Chalmette like it big. Located near an oil refinery (which provides many hungry customers), this diner offers huge helpings of staples, such as lima beans and rice, fried seafood, and the best macaroni and cheese on the planet. R&C usually stays open at least till midnight on weekends; call first.... *Tel 504/279–8323. 613 W. Bernard Hwy., Chalmette. No credit cards. $*

St. Ann's Deli. This friendly neighborhood diner is located right off busy Bourbon Street. It's a good bet for late night po-boys, especially on weekends, when it never closes.... *Tel 504/529–4421. 800 Dauphine St., French Quarter. $*

St. Charles Tavern. This 24-hour diner is a little dingy, but has a passable menu including seafood and steaks. It'll work fine at 3am.... *Tel 504/523–9823. 1433 St. Charles Ave., Garden District. $*

Siam Cafe. Vegetarian curries, spring rolls, great noodle dishes, and other Thai specialties are served late in the upstairs section of this local favorite. Seating is on the balcony and in the "Dragon's Den," where live bands play.... *Tel 504/949–1750. 435 Esplanade Ave., Faubourg Marigny. DC not accepted. $*

The Trolley Stop. Nobody ever calls the St. Charles streetcar a trolley. Who ever heard of "A Trolley Named Desire"? Nonetheless, this new 24-hour cafe is quickly becoming a local favorite, offering a huge selection of breakfasts, sandwiches, and dinners.... *Tel 504/523–0090. 1923 St. Charles Ave., Garden District. DC not accepted. $*

Vic's Kangaroo Cafe. This popular Downtown bar serves Australian food to complement its Australian beers and wines. This is certainly the only place in town for snag rolls, dog's eyes, and chook pies, which are served till the joint closes, usually about 3am on weekends.... *Tel 504/524–4329. 636 Tchoupitoulas St., Warehouse District. $*

NEW ORLEANS ⟋ LATE NIGHT DINING

down
and
dirty

Babysitters... While you're out sampling New Orleans's nighttime diversions, you can have **Accent Child Care** (tel 504/524–1227) or **Dependable Kid Care** (tel 504/486–4001 or 800/862–5806) keep an eye on the young 'uns.

Car rental... There are advantages to renting a car in this city, especially if you plan on being here for more than a couple of days. Why rent? First and foremost, the Quarter gets old after a while; you find yourself bumping into the same tourists on Bourbon Street, and that charming riverboat calliope starts to sound like Mississippi Muzak. With a car, however, you can explore the scenic Northshore, the bayous of the West Bank, and the many diverse neighborhoods around town. Most major car rental companies have facilities in both the downtown area and at the airport. (Tip: the airport rates are usually cheaper.) Some of the biggies are **Avis** (tel 800/831–2847 or 504/523–4317; 2024 Canal St., Downtown), **Budget** (tel 800/527–0700 or 504/467–2277; 1317 Canal St., Downtown), and **Hertz** (tel 800/654–3131 or 504/568–1645; 901 Convention Center Blvd., Downtown).

Driving around... Driving in New Orleans can be an educational experience. The only problem is, most of the lessons take place in the middle of an intersection. At corners, drivers inch perilously far into traffic. Nobody uses a turn signal. Crater-sized potholes send your steering wheel spinning. And in many neighborhoods, the only street signs are little, faded, narrow strips attached vertically to telephone poles. Really. Lane-changing is an adventure sport; Orleanians compete to see who can cover the greatest number of lanes most quickly. Be aware, though, that if you try to join in the fracas, you may have to contend with the New Orleans Police Department, and if you've ever seen *The Big Easy*, you know that's something you'd probably like to avoid. So drive patiently, defensively, and safely.

Emergencies... Dial **911** for emergency assistance. Hospitals with 24-hour emergency rooms include **Tulane University Medical Center** (tel 504/588–5711; 1415 Tulane Ave., Downtown), **Touro Infirmary** (tel 504/897–8250; 1401 Foucher St., Uptown), and the **Medical Center of Louisiana** (tel 504/568–2311; 1532 Tulane Ave., Downtown), known to locals as Charity Hospital.

Festivals and special events... Really, there are only two seasons in this town, and the other one is summer. This is the great equalizer: we all look and feel about the same when a bead of perspiration is trickling down the front of our nose. During the hottest months, nobody's really thinking about festivals or special events—we all just want to find the nearest room with air-conditioning. Summer notwithstanding, New Orleans is a city of feasts and fetes, and there's always a place at the table for one more. What follows is a compendium of some of New Orleans's best festivals, along with the most popular annual goings-on in outlying regions. The list is far from comprehensive: there just wasn't room for the "Celebration of the Giant Omelette," the "Shrimp and Petroleum Festival," or the "Cracklin' Festival." (For these and about two hundred other unusual events, write to: Louisiana Association of Fairs and Festivals, 601 Oak Lane, Thibodaux, LA, 70301–6537.) But to paraphrase Dr. John, if you pay attention to this calendar, it should help you be in the right place, at the right time.

January: The **Sugar Bowl** (tel 504/525–8374; New Year's Day) hits the Superdome like a ton of college linebackers. In addition to the big game, the event includes sundry athletic competitions, ranging from basketball to sailing. The other big event this month is January 6 or **Twelfth Night** (so called because the date is twelve nights after Christmas), when the Carnival season officially begins with the traditional ride of the Phunny Phorty Phellows down a St. Charles streetcar. The bakeries fill with King Cakes, parades start rolling everywhere, and all the thrift stores put their costume racks out front.

February: In this city, blasphemy and blessings are closely linked: **Mardi Gras** is the day before Ash Wednesday, which is determined by the church calendar (future dates of Mardi Gras are: 1997, February 11; 1998, February 24; 1999, February 16; 2000, March 7). In recent years, the city has been promoting **Lundi Gras**, the day before Mardi Gras, by sponsoring concerts in the Spanish Plaza. The music is good, but the event feels a little too organized to be Carnival. If you're in town during the weeks before Mardi Gras, don't fret: some of the best parades roll through town prior to Carnival Day. Check the daily paper for schedules and maps.

March: The **Louisiana Black Heritage Festival** (tel 504/861–2537; call for date) is a popular Audubon Zoo event that features traditional and contemporary R&B, gospel, and some rap acts, with a big-name headliner. The **Audubon**

Pilgrimage (tel 504/635–6330; third weekend), in St. Francisville, offers tours to antebellum homes that are normally closed to the public year-round. **St. Patrick's Day** parades, on or near March 17, are a blow-out for both the Irish and the Irish-at-heart. The wildest procession (it's more fun than most Mardi Gras parades) rolls through the residential Irish Channel neighborhood (tel 504/565–7080); and **Molly's at the Market** also throws a great French Quarter parade and party (tel 504/525–5169). **St. Joseph's Day**, March 19, is another much-celebrated feast day, especially by members of the city's Italian community, who build elaborate altars of food and sponsor a nighttime parade (tel 504/522–7294) through the French Quarter on the second Saturday of the month. **Super Sunday** is the name of the year's best Mardi Gras Indian gathering; the exact day of this parade of Indians and brass bands is a little hard to predict, but it usually takes place on a Sunday near St. Joseph's Day—check the daily paper or try calling WWOZ radio station (tel 504/568–1234) for info. **Earth Fest** (tel 504/581–4629; third or fourth weekend), at the Audubon Zoo, is a mainstream environmental fair with exhibitors ranging from Shell Oil to the Sierra Club, along with live music and entertainment. The **Islenos Festival** (tel 504/682–0862; third or fourth weekend), in nearby Chalmette, is a modest but fascinating cultural festival featuring Islenos food, crafts, and music. The **New Orleans Spring Fiesta** (tel 504/581–1367; last weekend) has a carriage parade and tours of historic homes for fans of the genteel South. The **Tennessee Williams Literary Festival** (tel 504/286–6680; usually last weekend) brings writers and readers out of the woodwork with an exceptional program of discussions, lectures, and theater, with a focus on Southern literature. UNO professor Kenneth Holditch also leads a fascinating literary walking tour of the Quarter. Events are centered around Le Petit Théâtre in the French Quarter.

April: There's nothing quite like **Easter** in the French Quarter for the chance to witness a mixture of the sacred and profane. After Sunday Mass in the St. Louis Cathedral, aristocrat ladies parade through the streets, passing beads and toys to oft-confused passersby. Meanwhile, just blocks away, the local transvestite population is out in full force for its own Easter bonnet parade. The **French Quarter Festival** (tel 504/522–5730; usually second weekend) kicks off the music festival season with numerous music stages throughout the Quarter; it's mainly geared to tourists, but the strong traditional jazz lineup appeals to local music fans also. The **New Orleans Jazz and Heritage Festival** (tel 504/522–4786; last weekend of April and first weekend of May), fondly known as Jazz Fest, brings literally hundreds of thousands of music lovers to the Fair Grounds for one of the world's biggest and brightest music events. Some of these folks escape the crowds by taking the two-hour drive to the smaller **Festival International de Louisiane** (tel 318/232–8086; last weekend) in Lafayette, which is devoted to the music of the world, especially that of Francophone countries.

May: The **Zoo-To-Do** (tel 504/861–2537; first Friday) is an annual society fund-raiser to benefit the Audubon Zoo, with fine food and finer music. The **Breaux Bridge Crawfish Festival** (tel 318/332–6655; first weekend), about a two-hour drive west of New Orleans, is another food-and-music combo that competes for crowds with Jazz Fest, offering one of the year's best schedules of Cajun and zydeco music. The **Greek Festival** (tel 504/282–0259) is small but fun; it's located in the Hellenic Cultural Center in New Orleans East. And **Zydeco Extravaganza** (tel 800/346–1958; Memorial Day weekend), in Lafayette, is one of the year's biggest zydeco dances, and definitely the coolest—the day and night event is held in the air-conditioned Blackham Coliseum.

June: **Zephyrfest** (tel 504/641–5672; usually first weekend) is New Orleans's own version of Lollapalooza, attracting about 20,000 fans to Marconi Meadows in City Park for a day and evening of top national alternative bands. The next weekend, butch cuts are traded for dreds, as **Reggae Riddums Festival** (tel 504/367–1313; second weekend) hits Marconi Meadows with national and local Caribbean acts. Warning: even after the sun goes down, these festivals can be steamy. The **French Market Tomato Festival** (tel 504/522–2621; first weekend) celebrates the Creole tomato season with free local bands and lots of free tomato samples. The month-long **Juneteenth Celebration** (tel 504/581–2245) honors the African-American holiday with gospel concerts, festivals, and parades. **Louisiana Bluesberry Festival** (tel 504/892–8650; usually third Saturday) is a small-town family festival with lots of fresh blueberries and even fresher local blues acts, such as J. Monque'D; it's well worth the scenic drive across Lake Pontchartrain to the Northshore. And **Carnaval Latino** (tel 504/523–9540; usually last week) attracts merengue and salsa dancers with a good roster of international and local Latin bands, playing near the French Quarter in Woldenberg Riverfront Park.

July: **Go Fourth on the River** (tel 504/522–5730) is a fairly decent Independence Day celebration, in Woldenberg Park, that features live music and fireworks. The **New Orleans Wine and Food Experience** (tel 504/529–WINE; last weekend) is a chance to strut up and down Royal Street with a wineglass in your hand, sampling vino and gawking at art in participating galleries and restaurants.

August: In case you haven't noticed, things are starting to slow down now, as the city turns into a giant steam bath. Have you ever wondered why people talk and walk a bit more leisurely in the South? Are you still wondering?

September: To get to two of the year's most popular music festivals, you have to take a two-hour drive west: The **Southwest Louisiana Zydeco Festival** (tel 318/942–2392; Saturday before Labor Day) is held near the small town of Plaisance, in a converted soybean field, while **Festivals Acadiens** (tel 800/346–1958; third weekend) is two days and nights of Cajun music in Girard Park in Lafayette. Back in New Orleans, **Weindorf New Orleans** (tel 504/522–5730; usually third weekend) is a smaller festival of German music and food in Washington Square in the Faubourg Marigny.

October: **Louisiana Jazz Awareness Month** (tel 504/522–3154 or 504/364–5995) is a month-long series of concerts, workshops, lectures, and exhibits that won't let you forget that New Orleans is the birthplace of jazz. The **Angola Prison Rodeo** (tel 504/655–4411; Sundays) is one of Louisiana's strangest offerings: an inmate rodeo in the maximum security prison recently made famous in the movie *Dead Man Walking*. **Art for Arts' Sake** (tel 504/528–3800; first Saturday), a benefit for the Contemporary Arts Center, has live music, new installations, and food from local restaurants. In recent years, the neighboring Julia Street galleries have been getting into the act, and this affair is turning into a giant neighborhood arts party. The **Louisiana Swamp Festival** (tel 504/861–2537; first two weekends) is the best Cajun and zydeco music fest in

New Orleans, with top bands playing under giant oak trees in the Audubon Zoo. The **New Orleans Film and Video Festival** (tel 504/523–3818; second Friday through third Sunday), which keeps growing every year, now presents over a hundred films and videos. These are mostly independent and foreign works, though a couple of major studios usually offer regional (or sometimes national) premieres of major films, and the director or stars often come to town for the occasion. The **Jeff Fest** (tel 504/888–2900; second weekend), in Lafreniere Park, is Jefferson Parish's grand attempt to prove that rockin' music festivals can happen in the suburbs, too. It had a shaky start in 1991, but hit its stride in recent years with a schedule emphasizing classic rock. The **Baton Rouge Blues Festival** (tel 800/LA–ROUGE; second or third weekend) is in Louisiana's capitol city, about an hour out of New Orleans. Finally, **Halloween** is an opportunity for people to stroll the French Quarter in our second-best costumes. (We reserve our finest for Mardi Gras.)

November: **Celebration in the Oaks** (tel 504/482–4888; Thanksgiving through New Year's Eve) offers some enchanting evenings in City Park, with thousands of webs of colored lights strung throughout Storyland and the Carousel Gardens. You can drive or walk through the park, or hop aboard the little trolley.

December: **New Orleans Christmas** (tel 504/522–5730; through the month) is the umbrella name for a variety of holiday affairs. Some of the largest ones—such as the parade—have been scrapped, for want of cash, but the season's spirit can still be found in various historic home tours, tree lighting ceremonies, and organized caroling. **Festival of the Bonfires** (tel 504/562–2300; usually second weekend), in the towns of Lutcher and Gramercy, about 30 miles out of New Orleans, is the state's most unique Christmas event: Locals set fire to large pyres along the levee, in order to light the way for St. Nick. Traffic can be heavy, so plan ahead. Finally, the year ends with a **New Year's Eve** countdown in Jackson Square, a kind of mini-Times Square event.

Music hotlines... The 24-hour **WWOZ Tower Records Second Line** (tel 504/840–4040) offers the *OffBeat* Live Wire Music Calendar as well as the WWOZ Community Calendar. The music listings come from *OffBeat* (see warning in "Newspapers and magazines," below).

For the jazzy happenings in town, try the **Louisiana Jazz Federation**'s reliable 24-hour jazz hotline (tel 504/364–5995), which is updated every Monday and Friday.

Newspapers and magazines... In early 1996, New Orleans' only daily newspaper, the *Times-Picayune*, quietly dropped its music club listings. The local music community stormed the paper with angry letters and phone calls. A month later, the newspaper, just as quietly, put the listings back in. In addition to this hard-won schedule, the *T-P* is the best source for daily Mardi Gras parade routes and other special events. Some people even turn to the obituaries to find out if there are any jazz funerals this week. On Friday, the "Lagniappe" insert runs detailed club listings and music features by critic Keith Spera, along with theater reviews, movie schedules, and other arts and entertainment info.

In the past couple of years, **Gambit Weekly** has cashed in its somewhat stodgy reputation to become a fresh voice in the local arts and entertainment scene. As a free alternative weekly, *Gambit*'s style is a bit more irreverent than what you'll find in the *T-P.* For an inside track, turn to the "24/7" section and check out the recommendations in the "Best Bets," "Rhythm & News," and Rich Collins' "Swell" column. You can find *Gambit* at many bars, restaurants, hotels, clubs, and shops around town. Also, be sure to pick up a free copy of **OffBeat**, a monthly music magazine that is distributed in the same locations, especially in music clubs. Widely considered to be the bible of local music, this is undoubtedly the town's best source for in-depth interviews and features on blues, jazz, rock, R&B, and zydeco. Warning: be careful of *OffBeat*'s listings, which inevitably aren't as up-to-date as the weekly or daily papers.

Where is another freebie, but it's hardly worth the bother. Available at hotels and in French Quarter shops, this monthly smothers the city in a viscous layer of uncritical praise, and can't be trusted for much besides phone numbers and addresses. Local mags for purchase include **New Orleans** and **Louisiana Life**, two reputable (but far from radical) monthly periodicals. The new kid in town is **Tribe**, a slick monthly that covers alternative culture, usually with some half-clad model on the cover. Other local periodicals are geared to target audiences, including **Aquí New Orleans** (Spanish language); the **Louisiana Weekly**

and the *New Orleans Tribune* (African-American);
Mature Times (age 50-plus); and *The Weekly Guide*,
Ambush, and *Impact News* (gay and lesbian).

Online information... A number of news groups and web
sites are devoted to all sorts of New Orleans topics, and
folks will be happy to give you more information than
you ever needed about crawfish, riverboat rides, and
French Quarter prostitution rings. A good way to reach
these is to get a link through *OffBeat*'s web page (http://
www.neosoft.com~offbeat). This site also has online
copies of *OffBeat* articles, and is the best way to quickly
access Jazz Fest's schedule. *Gambit* also runs an excellent
web site (http://www.gambit-no.com/).

Parking... The most difficult thing about driving in New
Orleans may be the end of your journey, when you have
to park. If you're in the French Quarter, you might as well
give up your search for the perfect space, and opt for a
parking lot (which should only set you back a few dollars
at night). Try the larger ones in Canal Place, or near
Tower Records on North Peters Street. If you choose to
park on the street, read all the signs. The most confusing
thing about parking in New Orleans is that several separate signs apply to the same space, and it takes a few sec-
onds to put all the information together. Pay close attention to the signs that limit non-resident parking to two
holidays. Conspiracy buffs insist that it's all a civic plan to
shake more parking ticket money from our pockets, but
anyone with a level head realizes that this town isn't efficient enough to hatch so elaborate a plot.

Public transportation... If you truly desire a streetcar,
it's best to ride it during the day. At night, the "Charley
Cars" (so called because they rumble down St. Charles
Avenue) run infrequently, and there's nothing like a 45-
minute wait at a downtown transit stop to sap your
enthusiasm. But if you can't delay the streetcar experience
till morning, pick up an evening car on Carondelet at
Canal Street and take it up to Riverbend, where you can
get a bite to eat at either Cooter Brown's or the Camellia
Grill (see Late Night Dining). But when you're done, it's
best to call a cab for your ride home.

Meanwhile, you can forget about buses. They run
infrequently, and only a native or a cartographer can figure out their twists and turns. One bus even announces
its destination as "Cemeteries" on the front—in the dark

of night in New Orleans, the sight of that bus lurching up the street toward you is pretty unnerving. If you insist on obtaining a public transit route, call the RTA's 24-hour **RideLine** (tel 504/248–3900).

Radio stations... For the best New Orleans music news— as well as the best New Orleans music—locals keep an ear tuned and a car button punched on 90.7 FM for **WWOZ**, a community radio station that serves up a steady diet of traditional R&B, jazz, zydeco, gospel, Cajun, and just about every other type of local music (except rock and rap). Listening to WWOZ deejays, such as the Governor, Mr. Jazz, John Sinclair, and Billy Dell, is one of the great pleasures of being in New Orleans. Unfortunately, the local NPR affiliate, **WWNO** (89.9 FM), doesn't offer much by way of local music or news, opting instead for a mostly greatest-hits classical format. The exception is announcer Fred Kasten's superior "Inside the Arts" program.

Taxis... The best solution for short-term transportation needs is the old stand-by: the taxi. In New Orleans, it's best to call ahead: most drive-by cabs you'll see are already on their way to pick up a fare. The hands-down favorite company in New Orleans is **United** (tel 504/522–9771 or 800/323–3303). Other recommended cab companies are **Checker-Yellow** (tel 504/943–2411) and **Liberty Bell** (tel 504/822–5974). The base fare is $2.10, plus 75 cents per person. Travel is 20 cents for each one-sixth of a mile or 40 seconds. It's customary to tip your drivers about 10%. Warning: if your driver seems a little too eager to take you straight to a favorite restaurant, sniff the air for the faint smell of kickback.

Tickets... For big shows, clubs such as the House of Blues sell advance tickets. For smaller shows, it's a good bet to get there early to get your hand stamped, and avoid the line, especially during peak seasons, such as Jazz Fest and Mardi Gras. For one-stop shopping for tickets for sports, music, theater, and just about any other major event (except a Pearl Jam show), **Ticketmaster** (tel 504/522–5555 or 800/488–5252) is the only game in town. **Tower Records** in the French Quarter (408 N. Peters St., French Quarter) has a Ticketmaster desk open until midnight. The ticket service will tack on a service charge (even higher if you charge by phone), so it may be worth it to get advance tickets at each venue's box office.

Walking around... Walking at night can be scary—and not the cute, ghoulish, Anne Rice kind of scary. Like many tourist destinations, New Orleans has more than a few robbers that specialize in finding stray tourists with video cameras and wads of cash. This shouldn't scare you away from any restaurants and music clubs listed in this book. But if you don't know where you're going, don't set out on your own at night into unfamiliar neighborhoods with some hand-scrawled directions. In general, observe common-sense rules that apply to walking in any city after dark: don't be alone, and do stick to populated, well-lit streets. When in doubt, call a taxi.